HOPE

HOPE

How street dogs taught
me the meaning of life

NIALL HARBISON

HarperElement
An imprint of HarperCollins*Publishers*
1 London Bridge Street
London SE1 9GF

www.harpercollins.co.uk

HarperCollins*Publishers*
Macken House, 39/40 Mayor Street Upper
Dublin 1, D01 C9W8, Ireland

First published by HarperElement 2023
This edition published 2024

24 25 26 27 28 LBC 6 5 4 3 2

© Niall Harbison 2023

Niall Harbison asserts the moral right to
be identified as the author of this work

Plate-section photographs courtesy of the author

A catalogue record of this book is available
from the British Library

ISBN 978-0-00-862724-9

Printed and bound in the USA

To my mum and dad, sister and brothers, my grannies, extended family and a handful of close friends who I've put through endless worry over the years because of my addictions, and who now rarely see me as I'm off saving dogs 24/7.

I am the person I am because of you, and I can only hope my actions now make you all proud. This is for you.

CONTENTS

PROLOGUE

Crouching down for a closer inspection of the tiniest little thing in front of me – barely a scrap of life, though the violent quivering certainly proved there was life – I winced. I couldn't help it. Then I let out the kind of long exhale you do – *oooooofffff* – when you can't really find the right words to describe what you're seeing.

You poor little bubba, I muttered under my breath, shaking my head in sorry disbelief.

There's always one that can still get to you, take you aback, however much you think you've seen it all. I must have come across hundreds and hundreds of dogs and puppies, in all kinds of sorry and horribly pathetic states, over the last couple of years since I've been living in Thailand. You feel so desperate for each and every one of them. And I have had to bury countless of those who don't make it. Yet to some extent, you get hardened to it. You have to really, or you couldn't carry on.

Life just isn't easy for the street dogs here, with no owner to take care of them, no place to call home. No safe haven to take shelter. No one to look out for them when they're sick. Every single meal is hard won. With no idea where the next one is coming from. The fact that they soldier on, mainly quite happily, living in the moment and grateful for their lot, blows my mind.

But occasionally, when you get a little puppy who is poorly like this one in front of me, however hardened you've become to the street dogs' plight, it can still tear at your heart strings.

This wee little mite here, in my makeshift office in the middle of the Ko Samui jungle, would make anyone want to cry. Barely the size of a melon, I guessed he was just four or five weeks old.

He had huge, dark puppy-dog eyes, floppy ears and four legs, but otherwise, more than anything else he was really just a little ball of … mank. Admittedly that's hardly a medical term, and I'm certainly no vet, but it was just impossible to describe him in any other more technical way.

Ah, you poor little baby, I soothed. I had the urge to stroke him, show him some tenderness and affection, yet his entire skin was so desperately red raw I honestly wasn't sure which patch of his body to touch that wouldn't just cause further agony for the little guy. He was entirely lacking in any fur, nothing to keep him warm or protect him from the elements. Almost every millimetre of the poor little fella was covered in scabs, horribly sore open wounds and yukky, scaly skin.

What the hell has happened to you, little one?

Gently, I placed the lightest finger-touch on his front paw, which seemed the safest place to aim for. I needed to let him know somehow that I was there for him. I wasn't the enemy. I was a friend. And I wanted to help make him better.

He was shaking so hard. Was it from cold? Fear? Illness? I wasn't sure how his tiny body – small enough to fit in the palm of my hand – was even coping with the force of such violent quivering. His whimpers were so weak you had to strain to hear them.

Hey buddy, we've got you now, I whispered, stroking his front paw on the same tiny patch of skin that looked like it was either about to explode with pus, ooze with blood or possibly even just fall off.

I looked up in horror towards my friend, Rod, who'd brought him in to me.

'Jesus Christ, Rod.' I grimaced as Rod stood above me while I crouched over the puppy.

'I know, mate,' said Rod, shaking his head. 'He's in a bad way all right.'

Like me, Rod is a passionate animal lover and we'd done many rescues together since I'd been living here. Rod had found this pathetic little creature all by himself, by the side of the road, wandering out from a bush where he had probably been scrounging for scraps of food.

God knows how he'd got there. I imagine he'd had siblings who hadn't made it. God knows how he'd survived this long. As is often the case, we didn't know any of the pup's back story. But Rod had scooped him up and brought him in to see if anything could be done to ease his suffering.

'I don't know whether this one's going to make it,' I said. We had absolutely no idea what was wrong with his skin, what had caused it to be in such a terrible state. It was mange, I was pretty sure of that. Mange, a disease caused by mites, is not uncommon in this part of the world. It causes intense itching and as a result of all the scratching, animals suffer open sores, scabs and hair loss. But this little one's seemed worse somehow. The skin infections were just so severe. I had to try and help him.

Fetching the softest blanket I could find from my office, and as gently as I could, I scooped him up, hoping the blanket would provide some protective cushioning from the sores. But he let out the most heartbreaking little yelp where he was clearly hurting, looking up at me with big, pleading eyes.

Shhh, it's OK, I soothed. You can't help feeling guilty that you've caused more pain, even if you are trying to help.

He was red raw, with pus seeping out from some of the nastier sores. He hadn't even been able to sit still because the pressure from the weight of his little body on the hard floor was too much to bear. He'd been wriggling about trying to find a spot of respite. At least now I had him cocooned like a little baby, all wrapped up in the blanket.

It was getting dark outside. I knew if Rod hadn't found him that night, this pup wouldn't have made it through to dawn.

I wrapped him in a little bundle, big eyes and snout clear to breathe, and found him a quiet corner of the office to rest for the night, placing a soft toy next to him. I often bring the pups and dogs soft toys, a bit like you would for a baby. Some dogs love them, not all are interested, but even if they're not fussed it makes me feel better somehow. Treating them with kindness, showing them love. I wondered what had happened to this one's mummy, and how frightened he must have been when that protection had been taken away from him.

Slowly his shivering eased, and his eyes – once wide with fear – began closing. I could tell he'd been in a high adrenaline, 'flight or fight' mode. When you're close to death, that's what your body does, it's part of the survival instinct. But now the poor wee mite was just absolutely battered, and all the stress hormones had left his little body.

I've seen this many times when dogs are at death's door like this. Once they know they are safe, they start relaxing, which sounds good but actually can mean they go sharply downhill, healthwise. That's when you can lose them.

We fed him some basic medicines, to relieve the pain and to reduce some of the swelling from the sores, which I hoped would aid in getting a restful sleep. And tomorrow morning I would be with him at the vet's first thing. I vowed that if he'd made it through the night, and the vet had some optimism he was a goer, I'd cook him some beautiful steak and fresh mackerel.

I'd come across a dog with terrible skin like this before. We'd called him Derek, and he was a wonderful, sweet-natured animal who we all insanely adored (and still do – you'll get to meet Derek properly later!). I'd had the most amazing results by feeding Derek fatty fish like mackerel and showing him love, affection and patience. Over time, Derek's horrific skin disorder had healed, and was now totally cleared up. He's a gorgeous dog and I'm so happy we stuck with him and watched him blossom with good health and a hilarious personality.

I really hoped that with some medicines, time, high-quality nutrition and a whole lot of love, it might do the trick for this little fella too.

'You get home now, Rod,' I told my friend. He looked almost as exhausted as the pup. Dog rescuing is hard work, emotionally draining and very long hours. Rod is one of the most dedicated animal lovers I've ever met.

'So what will we call the newbie then, Niall?' asked Rod, as he picked up his car keys to drive home.

I looked at the bundle who seemed to be snoozing next to me.

'Let's call him Rodney,' I said. 'After you. And then let's hope this little Rodney will be inspired to get better like Derek did.' I've always been a fan of *Only Fools and Horses*, and the thought of having a Del Boy and a little Rodders now for company made me smile.

After Rod left, I crouched down over his sleeping little namesake and – manky skin or not – I placed the gentlest of kisses on his tiny black snout, willing him to make a recovery. I reckoned it was fifty–fifty whether he'd still be with us in the morning. But I wouldn't be leaving him alone now.

I gave his tiny paw a few more strokes and prepared myself for a long night ahead.

ONE

WHEN I WAS A BOY ... AND A TROUBLED TEEN

You're no doubt an animal lover like me if you've picked up this book. But have they always been your special friends?

Today, I'm a bald Irish guy who spends every waking hour in the company of dogs (and most of my sleeping hours dreaming of them, if I'm honest). So you might assume I've always had special dogs in my life and shared bonds with them since I was knee-high to a grasshopper, but that's not the case. Growing up, they were not part of my life at all.

I was raised as an only child in Brussels. There was just me, Mum and Dad for years. And we were happy. My mum, Kathleen, and my dad, Ronan, were very young when they got together, both Catholic and from neighbouring villages in County Tyrone, in Northern Ireland. They'd met at some local dance. Which sounds old fashioned compared to today's dating apps, but when you're in the depths of a rural fishing community, that's just how you met someone.

Mum's family worked hard and were good people, salt of the earth. From the photos I've seen, she was a real stunner in her day, and my dad, who was hard working and ambitious, was totally smitten. They married in the village church and I came along in 1979 when Mum was 19 and Dad was 22, their first born and only child together.

Northern Ireland – with The Troubles then raging – was not a great place to bring up a kid. So when I was still a baby and Dad was offered a civil servant job, with the recently established European Commission in Brussels, we moved over there. It was a real opportunity for my parents to have a better life.

We lived in an ordinary semi-detached house in a middle-class suburb popular with the ex-pat community. It was modest really, one of hundreds of commuter homes, but to me it was magical – my own castle. I had my own bedroom and a wall in the garden to play tennis against, a garage where I kept my bicycle, and plenty of room to practise my football skills.

My early childhood at least was completely idyllic. I remember a lot of happiness and love, with friends coming over for barbecues, regular football practice and kids birthday parties. I was football obsessed as a lad. I supported Manchester United and Diego Maradona was my hero. I was fairly decent too; not good enough to be a professional but I'd spend every minute of my free time kicking a ball around, with hours and hours spent focusing on improving. In hindsight, perhaps that was an early sign of my addictive nature. I've never been diagnosed officially, but I'm pretty certain if I was in the school system today I'd have been labelled as having ADHD and put into classes for kids with special needs. I was always full of energy and could never sit still, with my brain darting all over the place. I haven't changed much on that front, to be fair!

While Dad was the breadwinner, Mum stayed at home raising me, which I guess was typical of the 1980s. Still, it can't have been easy for her, being so far from home, away from her big family, and having a baby to look after while she was still so young herself. Cheap flights with Ryanair hadn't yet become a thing, so zipping back and forth to County Tyrone wasn't an option. But every long summer holiday and at Christmas we'd go back home to see the family. Mum had seven brothers and sisters so there were lots of cousins to play with, and we'd scramble around the fields playing soldiers and running around with my grandmother's lovely cocker spaniel, Pickles.

With no siblings, I was always independent, a natural introvert and a loner. I was perfectly content spending hours by myself. I'm still like that today. Social situations have given me anxiety my whole life, and still do.

Mum and Dad were great friends with another Irish couple who'd moved over to Belgium at the same time as us, and their son Sean was exactly my age. He was, and still is today, my best mate in the world. You could say I was spoilt really, with my nice life going to the smart international school with all the other ex-pat kids in Brussels. You pick up languages so quickly at that age, and I soon became fluent in French and Flemish, though I still speak with an Irish accent today.

Thailand is now my forever home. But for a long time I had no idea where 'home' was for me. I never felt home was anywhere particular really. Not Northern Ireland, or Belgium, or even Dublin, where I spent years later. I'm grateful for the opportunity I had to experience a more cosmopolitan, European type of life growing up, feasting on mussels and chips, and mixing with people from all over the world.

There was definitely a more relaxed attitude around alcohol on the Continent. Kids were allowed to try sips of beer or wine with their families, and it would be normal for teenagers to have some beers after playing football, or be in a pub from age 14 onwards, with no one particularly frowning at that. The binge-drinking culture in the UK and Ireland is unfortunately infamous across the world, but it wasn't like that in Belgium when I was growing up. Mum liked some wine with dinner and Dad would have a few beers in the garden, but neither parent was what you'd call a massive boozer. So my eventual dependency on alcohol can't be blamed on inheriting it from them.

What I *did* carry a lot of blame around for, for many destructive years in later life, was my parents splitting up. I blamed Mum, I blamed Dad, I blamed myself.

Everything in my life until I was 13 had been perfect. I was spoilt, safe and happy. Their divorce was a seismic event in my life. I had no idea my parents were even having marital issues. I don't recall rows. But one horrible night, I was in my bedroom doing homework (or rather, not doing my homework) when I heard a commotion going on downstairs. Something serious was going on. The front door slammed. I heard Dad on the phone, crying.

'Dad?' I called, standing at the top of the stairs.

'Come down here Niall, I need to talk to you.'

My bare feet took slow steps down the stairs, a funny knotted feeling forming in my tummy. There, in my living room, stood my big, strong dad, my superhero, my life protector. He looked ashen, broken. There were tears in his reddened eyes.

What the hell …?

'Your mum,' he said, voice breaking. 'Your mum's left, Niall.'

Left? Where?

'What do you mean?' I replied, struggling to understand these peculiar, alien words coming out of Dad's mouth.

'Your mum has left us, Niall. She's gone off with another man.' Then Dad sat down on the sofa and sobbed.

My mind thought backwards, scrambling for clues. I did remember an argument a few days earlier, but I'd shrugged it off; I'd kept playing football, reading my books, keeping myself entertained. I was hitting puberty and no doubt girls of my own age were more on my mind. I wasn't thinking about Mum, she was always just there.

'She's coming back later though, right, Dad?'

'No, son.' Dad stared at the ground. 'She's not coming back.'

And she didn't.

Mum walked out in December 1992 and I've hated Christmas ever since.

With no mobile phones back then, I had no contact with Mum for weeks. Initially I was packed off to Sean's house for a 'holiday'. Then taken out of school and sent to Ireland for the Christmas break. The family were kind, but no one talked to me about what was going on.

Mum was gone? She hadn't even said goodbye …

There was a huge amount of stuff to be processed. I couldn't get my 13-year-old head around it at all. Instead, I buried it away.

A few weeks later, back in Brussels, I finally saw Mum. She was very apologetic, trying to explain that there were other reasons behind why she left. She reassured me she loved me very much, as did Dad. They meant well, they said the right things, but I didn't understand any of it. It was awkward, we struggled to talk properly. I shrugged off her hugs.

I don't know how a 13-year-old kid *should* deal with that situation, but how I reacted was to start acting out. A rebellious little fecker is what I became. Some kind of self-destructive nature had been ignited.

A couple of days after that miserably confusing Christmas break, I tried my first cigarette. One of the bolder kids from school, a cocky lad, had heard about Mum and Dad's split. The ex-pat community was small, gossipy.

'What's going on then?' he asked.

I mumbled what I knew. Mum had left with another guy. I was living with my dad.

'Ah shit,' he sympathised. 'Why don't you try one of these?' he said, waving a packet of Lucky Strikes at me.

Fuck it, why not be bad? Everything was shit now anyway.

Lighting up and inhaling was, of course, like everyone's first experience of smoking – revolting. It made me cough and hurt the back of my throat. But that unpleasant sensation mirrored exactly how I felt inside. It was horrible yet perfectly so.

After the split, Dad was always particularly generous with pocket money. So I'd spend the cash on cigarettes and soon started nicking them from the supermarket too, as much for the thrill as anything else. It's crazy to imagine it now, but there was even a smokers' corner at school in Brussels, where kids, with permission from their parents, were allowed to go and legitimately light up. And so began a decades-long smoking habit.

I'd also started enjoying beers and cider. I liked the buzz it gave me. For someone so shy like me, with social anxiety, it loosened me up, made me more chatty. I felt my confidence grow.

In the local village there was even a vending machine for cans of beer, so for 20 Belgian francs you could get out a tin of alcohol as easily as buying a can of Coke. We soon worked out you could put a small hand inside so you didn't even have to put the cash in.

During the week I stayed at home with Dad. It never felt quite the same without Mum there; it was like the joy and comfort and security had upped sticks with her. I always suspected Dad dreamed of them getting back together and rekindling the marriage. It was a confusing, painful time for everyone. But Dad looked after me, cooked the dinners, and was a loving father, which can't have been easy while holding down his EC job.

I saw Mum on the weekends. Her and Andreas – the new man she'd left Dad for – had moved in together, and their apartment was close enough for me to cycle to. I didn't always love going though. Mum had met Andreas in an office where they worked and they'd been having an affair for several months before she left Dad. I got on with Andreas as best I could, but adolescence wasn't a happy time. Around then I also developed an interest in gambling.

It started with a simple dice game organised by the school for a charity fundraiser. I got totally addicted that day, begging Dad for more francs to play again and again and again. I could see that 'the house' always won, but kids happily threw more cash away anyway. So I set up my own little casino at school, using the same rules. This time I was 'the house', not the school or charity. Until the teachers cottoned on and closed it down, there'd be ten kids crowding around to play every lunchtime. I was raking in a ridiculous amount of kids' pocket money and developing quite an entrepreneurial spirit.

From then on, I was always on to the next bit of trouble at school, dreaming up the next big scheme. I didn't care about getting into trouble. I had ideas about becoming a journalist at some stage, so I invested in a Dictaphone, supposedly to record conversations. Instead, what I recorded was the school bell. At the end of class, an electronic bell signalled time was up, so once I'd taped this, I played it fifteen minutes before the actual end of class – getting us all out early. Result.

Another prank was messing around with people's homework diaries, scrawling 'Mr O'Neill is a wanker' on one. I was constantly in the headteacher's office. And because I kept pissing around, I didn't pass the exams needed to progress to the next year. It was common enough for a pupil to move down a year. But I ended up being put back a year, then another one, and then another one. So by the age of 15, and a growing lad, there I was in a class with all the little 12-year-old boys. I felt like I was in a ridiculous comedy film. I probably could have done the work had I bothered to apply myself. But I was wild and ungovernable by then. It was agreed all round that I'd be better off leaving the school.

My parents then found a stricter boarding school establishment for me. My behaviour didn't exactly improve. I was always pushing the limits. I created mayhem by short-circuiting the morning alarm clock for both our dorm and the teacher in charge of getting us up. We all slept in and had the best day ever! The other kids treated me like a hero. That school was full of misfits like me. We all smoked and we all hit the beers on the Friday night train back to our families. Being in trouble was the least of my worries.

My biggest concern was Mum. She dutifully came to all my football matches, and we would have a nice bonding time together in the evenings, sometimes even sharing the odd beer. She'd got a new job and worked really hard to make her home nice for me. But things with Andreas were not good at all.

After they'd moved in together he'd become physically abusive. The bruises became more frequent, and my mum's excuses like 'I walked into the door' or 'I tripped down the stairs' became ever more flimsy.

I was scared of Andreas, and scared for Mum. I hated myself that I wasn't able to help her. I'd stay in my room pretending the rows – her crying, the dreadful noise of bangs and yells and whacks – weren't really happening. Mainly the rows seemed to involve his jealousy: if she dared to go anywhere without him, or have any life outside of him, he saw it as a threat. It wasn't that he was a big drinker, but he would go off on one and then lash out at her. I felt full of self-loathing that I wasn't protecting her. Instead, I hid or went out with mates and drank beer after beer to try and blot out the misery.

Like many abusers, Andreas would apologise and sweet-talk Mum and persuade her to stay, promising it wouldn't happen again. And for a while it wouldn't. Some days it felt normal, but I'd be on permanent tenterhooks. And sure enough, the violence would always return at some stage.

One time I heard the argument picking up heat from my room and crept down the hallway to the living room. I hovered outside. *Should I knock on the door? Make a noise from outside? Should I burst in?* I dithered, uncertain what to do, then walked in.

There was Mum on the sofa with him on top of her clutching something that looked like a lamp in his fist, wielding it in her face. They both stopped and stared at me. I stared back at them, eyes wide in horror. I retreated to my room and I remember thinking, *Well, I've stopped it this time, I've saved her.* I also remember thinking that life could never be as bad as this again, whatever happened in the future.

The next day Andreas took me out for a long walk, with some bullshit excuse. There was some sob story involving his own parents who had hit him. But I wasn't really listening. I felt I just had to go along with it, however I felt towards him. He was an idiot, but he was also a big fully grown man, I was still a skinny kid. He could have beaten my arse, for sure. I might have 'saved' Mum that time I walked in, but there were other injuries to come for her, including a cracked eye socket. He was a scumbag, all right.

Mum stayed with him for years and I was 16 when they had a child together, my sister Veronica. The abuse calmed down a bit when Mum was taking care of the baby, who I loved as much as I loathed the monster that was Andreas. Eventually, long after I'd fled the nest, she plucked up the courage to leave him, thank God. But it haunted me for many years.

While I wasn't acting out at home, my behaviour at school got worse. There was a particularly authoritarian teacher at my boarding school who I kept clashing with. At night time, I'd take geography books to read in bed. Reading about the outside world was an escape for me. One night, he found me reading by torchlight and confiscated the book and put me on suspension. I'm not an angry person by nature, but that time I lost the plot completely.

'Fuck you, you fucking prick!' I yelled furiously, among every other expletive I could possibly muster. 'I'm trying to teach myself things here, you can stick your fucking school up your arse!' I was fuming. I'd been at the boarding school for a year when they too asked me to leave.

So that's how I found myself at 17 years of age with no qualifications, totally clueless about what to do with my life, and ill equipped for adulthood.

TWO

KITCHEN WORK, A RECIPE FOR DISASTER FOR A BUDDING ALCOHOLIC ...

Mum was always supporting and loving, but she had baby Veronica to take care of now.

My lovely dad was never angry at me, though he had every reason to be. I'm sure he was desperately disappointed and worried, but he wanted me to get a trade, a means to earn a living in the future. So while the rest of my mates were planning where to go to university, Dad encouraged me to sign up for a catering college in Dublin. He was a keen cook, and at some stage I'd shown an interest. I'd often pick up one of his old recipe books and discovered making even a simple chicken pasta, like the kind Dad made, was quite therapeutic. All that chopping, stirring and creating something tasty helped to calm my bumble-bee mind.

So that was that. I flew over to Ireland for the interview feeling ridiculous in one of my dad's old suits, desperately trying to learn the names of kitchen equipment on the flight. God knows what I thought they were going to quiz me on. I needn't have worried because I got accepted at the Dublin College of Catering, which meant saying a sad goodbye to my best mate Sean as well as Kate, my girlfriend. Kate and I had been seeing each other for a few months, and one of the nicest things anyone has ever done for me was her organising a surprise going away party for me. We talked about making the relationship work with her in Belgium and me in Dublin, but the distance soon put paid to that.

That summer before the course started I worked in a restaurant in Northern Ireland while I stayed at my granny's. I earned one pound an hour – which was probably illegal – plating up turkey and ham for wedding guests, and getting shouted orders as I mashed potatoes. I loved it. This was miles better than boring school, and I felt so proud being handed a little brown envelope containing £50 at the end of the week. Feeling those notes and pound coins that I'd earned all by myself was priceless.

I'd spend it all on cider, Hooch alcopops, fags, and bags of chips. I'd met new friends from work and we'd go out, all excited young lads together. One time after too many beers, I lobbed a rock into a public fountain, then pretended I could only speak French to the policeman who caught me. Another time I danced on top of a car. Granny gave me a stern talking-to, I can tell you.

I tried weed for the first time too. Just a few puffs on someone's joint made me pull a 'whitie'. That put me off drugs for a while, but the booze appetite had truly set in.

Suddenly I felt a lot more grown-up. I didn't want to mess everything up like I had at school. By the time I started at the catering college I was determined to make something of myself. The course wasn't up to much in all honesty, but thanks to the summer job and my obsessive reading of cookery books, I'd enough confidence to walk straight in the back door at one of the city's few Michelin-starred restaurants, Peacock Alley, and land a (very lowly) job.

Every night after college, I'd head to Peacock Alley and get grafting. This was a whole other world from the wedding venue. It was the city's best restaurant back then, with a kitchen full of twenty-four sweary, hairy, testosterone-fuelled chefs, effing and jeffing as they wielded vast knives and big pans. And every time there was some big event in Dublin, all the celebrities like Ronan Keating and Mariah Carey flocked here. The glitz and glamour just fascinated me.

All the grunt work was my duty, the shitty chores like removing the spinach stalks, peeling garlic, making garnishes. If I dared to stray from the tiny bit of work-bench I was allocated, I'd literally get punched in the ribs. Jesus, the filthy language in that kitchen! That was an education in itself. It was a hotbed of misogynistic, tough-man types and I was the skinny little pasty-faced foreign kid. But I loved every second of that crazy environment, soaking up the skills like a sponge.

Two of the French chefs slagged me off one time. 'That fucking kid is clueless!' one cried. To be totally honest, I've never been a technically great cook. But I was cheeky enough to banter with the big guys. How I enjoyed answering back with a perfect French accent and seeing their faces drop. They soon came to accept me for my enthusiasm rather than my ability.

The head chef was a charismatic giant of a guy called Conrad Gallagher, a bit of a Gordon Ramsay type. At 6 ft 6 in, he'd stand there at the pass – the part where the kitchen food is handed over to the front-of-house staff – nodding at all the famous people while he was busily roaring orders at us. He was hot headed for sure, throwing plates across the kitchen if something wasn't up to his exacting standards. You just had to stay off his radar and work hard. I was a bit cheeky with him, never rude but not intimidated, and he sort of warmed to me. Everybody was terrified of his moods, but I'd diffuse his temper by teasing him. 'Come on, Conrad, where's the bloody potatoes?' I'd grin. He'd pretend to be outraged, then give me a little wink.

Sixteen-hour days were normal, and I saw proper grown men crying, broken by the brutal pace of the place. But I was young and keen to learn and somehow survived there until I'd graduated from the catering college. By then the diploma meant nothing to me. In the catering industry, if somebody wants to see if you can cook, they simply put you in a kitchen for four hours. They don't care about certificates. Still I was pleased to finally get one thing in my life, to make Dad proud. At last I'd stuck something out.

But if I was working hard these years, then I was playing even harder. Finishing a long shift at 11 pm meant I was buzzing, ready to party. Sean was back in Ireland by then, as were other school mates who'd come to study at university in Dublin. I'd meet them after work, hell bent on 'catching up' with their boozing.

My sophisticated tipple of choice in those days? Double vodka and Lucozade, or a triple vodka topped up with Smirnoff Ice. In a bid to get as drunk as humanly possible before the 2 am closing time, I'd stagger around clutching three drinks at any one time. When you urgently want to get smashed, there's no point wasting time by drinking beer, is there?

Generally it was mission to get drunk accomplished, and I'd end up way more blasted than Sean and the lads. But I wasn't concerned about my urgency to booze; binge-drinking was just accepted. There were nights where I had half an hour's sleep and then went into work. No one batted an eyelid.

And that gambling instinct I'd shown at school? Well, soon I was losing wages down the betting shops. Horses, greyhounds, bingo, footballing bets, it was all a thrill.

It was a chef who urged me to try my first line of cocaine. Cocaine use is rife in the catering industry. It gives you the energy for those crazy hours. I was nervous though about drugs, and actually managed to resist for several years. 'Come on, don't be a pussy!' they'd jeer, waving a bag of white powder and rolled-up banknotes in my face. Eventually, I gave in to peer pressure.

I also tried my first Ecstasy tablet around then too. After saying no for so long, I found myself agreeing to neck one in a ropey old Dublin nightclub. Half an hour later I was grinning maniacally. 'Oh my God,' I raved, off my tits. 'You guys are not lying. This is *amazing*!' I spent the rest of the night smiling, loving my sky-high confidence and dancing to techno music.

After that night I would go through little spells with drugs, like two or three weekends taking pills, but then I wouldn't touch them for six months because I knew it was too dangerous for someone like me. Already I was wary of my 'darker side' – I one hundred per cent knew that I had an addictive personality.

It was also around this time I started getting depression and anxiety. There is a strong link between mental health and drink and drug abuse, but I genuinely did not know that at the time. In fact, I didn't even know what depression or anxiety was. People weren't talking about it back in the 1990s, and certainly not young guys, in the way we might do now.

So I didn't link my dark moods to the lifestyle I was embracing. The post blowout, big night anxiety could be crippling some days. It would start with a tense jaw. Then I'd be too nervous to go to the shops or even step outside. I wouldn't be able to sleep.

The anxiety – and the drinking – escalated sharply when I was 21 and Conrad made me head chef at his latest restaurant, Lloyd's Brasserie. I was totally underqualified to do it and completely out of my depth. My family were really proud of me, the boy with no qualifications had actually achieved something. This made the nerves even worse. I felt like a fraud. I didn't know what I was doing. Soon all the staff hated me because they felt I shouldn't have had the job, they should. I didn't feel I could confide in anyone.

Instead, I just turned to alcohol to ease the anxiety … which of course made it worse. Once the 'relaxant' effect of the first drink had worn off, I kept having to drink more to chase it. And all that booze was like pouring fuel on my fears.

I had my first real panic attack when I went on holiday with a girlfriend, a really lovely girl called Sabrina who worked in the restaurant while she was studying. We were on a package holiday to Spain when I suddenly developed this horrific chest pain.

'I think we're gonna have to go to the hospital,' I cried, convinced I was dying.

The doctors checked everything and gave me some pills to calm me down but basically discharged me with a clean bill of health. Over the course of my twenties I was hospitalised five times with these same symptoms: a tightening chest, pains shooting down my arm, struggling to breathe. But the ECG was always clear. No one ever told me it was a panic attack. I genuinely believed for years I had some kind of underlying cardiac issue. It seems crazy I know, but I still never put any of it down to my chaotic partying lifestyle.

It didn't help that on the day before we were due to go on that holiday, I also lost 600 euros – money that we had been saving up – on gambling. I'd blown the whole lot in one afternoon and had to scramble around for a loan.

My bookies addiction was quietly ticking away in the background of my life. Those were the sorts of shitty things I would do, like failing to turn up somewhere because I was drunk or hungover; and Sabrina, like any self-respecting person would, dumped me.

'I can't continue like this,' she tearfully told me in the car. 'Not if you keep drinking, Niall.'

She was the first person to seriously suggest I had a drinking problem. And she certainly wasn't the last girlfriend to finish with me because of it.

After it all ended with Sabrina, I was miserable. I hated my job as head chef and woke up with severe anxiety every day. Sean and some other lads, Barry and Cillian, were now graduating and planning a trip to Australia. With little left to keep me in Dublin, I decided to quit work and join them.

I got employed in a kitchen out there easily enough, and the four of us rented a flat in Melbourne. All Irish lads, all drinking and smoking weed and up for the craic. It seemed the perfect place to get over a break-up. I threw myself into partying.

There was a 24/7 nightclub called Revolver. I went there one Friday and I didn't leave until Sunday evening. I took fifteen Ecstasy pills that weekend, washed down with gallons of rum and Coke. As you might imagine, the come-down wasn't pretty. I didn't get out of bed for five days, failed to show up at work and lost my job. The guys – who weren't into pills themselves – thought it was all hilarious. But they had no idea what an ugly place the inside of my head was. Even a trip to the toilet required three hours of psyching myself up to simply walk across the hallway.

There were plenty of other chef jobs to be had. Yet each time I'd last three months before a booze bender led to the sack. I'd laugh it off. 'I didn't want the job anyway,' I'd shrug to mates. It was always the drink. I was a shambles, making drunken calls to Sabrina, who'd very much moved on with her life.

I knew I wanted to change, but I'd lost my way.

The world wide web was just creeping into our lives, and sat in a small internet cafe I researched my options, stumbling upon working the ski seasons. I could cook, I wanted to snowboard, why not head to the mountains? Fancying a change of scenery, I headed to the Alps.

Working as a head chef in an English-run hotel there, all I had to do was churn out a basic level breakfast, afternoon tea and dinner. I could do that with my eyes closed. Which freed up all my time for snowboarding and the apres-ski scene. Within a couple of weeks, I wasn't bothering with the boarding at all, instead saving my energy for the partying. It was carnage, frankly.

Because the cooking required was so undemanding, I didn't see the harm in a few beers while I made a chicken casserole … or indeed cooked the breakfasts. For the first time I was even drinking beer at 7 am.

What's the harm?

Working a ski season, it turned out, is a gift to anyone with alcohol issues. Afternoon pints, hot wine, whiskey coffees – the opportunities to get on it were ample. Plus every week a new bunch of good-looking girls arrived. You can see how the cycle went. It was debauched, and not particularly happy. Before the season was up, I fell out with the boss and quit. I was still running from my responsibilities and the drink demons had firmly taken root.

THREE

ALL AT SEA

Working on yachts was my next great idea. To break into that world you needed to go 'dock walking', which was basically going up and down the docks handing in your CV while trying to find a season of employment.

I got my foot in the door and started off on a small 50-metre boat, then over a couple of years worked my way up to the bigger ones. The level of wealth was insane, even these so-called smaller boats would have cost sixty grand a week to hire. As for the bigger ones, we're talking millions.

It was brilliant because I could earn so much money working on them – 4,000 euros a month, plus tips on top. It's a really good way for people to save up cash, as all your board and lodgings are free. Even I couldn't drink all that away, and gambling wasn't an option on board so I invested some of my wages in stocks and shares.

One of the first jobs I had was working for a really nice businessman from Malta. I was his private chef, travelling with him to his mansion as well as his yacht. Jesus, his parties were on a whole other level! I cooked for his New Year's Eve bash in Green Park, London, and all his closest friends and guests. That evening we ended up in a crazily flamboyant nightclub dancing with around 3,000 topless men. It was mental but fun, and of course I got hammered consistently. Here I was, aged 23, my head turned by the sheer money these people had. It was all so dazzling to me.

After that, I landed a job on the billionaire Paul Allen's mega yacht, the 126-metre long *Octopus*. Paul was the guy who founded Microsoft with Bill Gates. The eighteen months I worked for him were crazy times. There was a swimming pool, a basketball court, a cinema and a wine bar on board, as well as a sailing yacht and a submarine.

I'd be downstairs below deck mainly, working out the logistics of ordering food and sorting supplies. Paul was very introverted and would mostly communicate by email, even though he was just upstairs on the yacht. He never wanted to pick his meal from a menu in advance, he wanted to see it first. So I'd have to create about ten dishes at every meal for him to choose what he fancied. He liked ice cream, so we'd have the freezer stocked with every imaginable flavour. One time, the one he wanted was the only one we didn't have, peach. When you're very rich, people treat you differently. Rather than just tell Paul, who would probably have happily chosen another, instead someone was packed off on a helicopter to find the peach flavour. That one tub of ice cream would effectively have cost thousands of bucks.

Sushi fish was flown in from Japan, truffles from France and buffalo mozzarella from Italy. Sustainability wasn't exactly on the agenda back then, but when you're that wealthy, that's how you can live, I guess. He kept not one but two helicopters on the boat, though he was decent and always made sure the staff got to use them if they needed to.

I once cooked a huge barbecue on the beach for Bill Gates' 50th birthday party and remember overhearing a chat Bill and his then wife Melinda were having. I was surprised by how nice and normal they seemed, talking about their kids' horse riding and how they were doing at school. Bill was clearly a genius, but so friendly; he'd chat to me as I was serving up his steak, then he wouldn't see me for six months but would still greet me with a 'Hey, Irish!' I couldn't believe he'd remembered.

We went all over the world. Anyone who was anyone came on the yacht, from royalty to big name rappers, movie stars like Angelina Jolie and Cuba Gooding Junior, sports stars like Lance Armstrong, and mega-rich socialites like Paris Hilton. There was a recording studio on the yacht, so I'd see pop stars like Shakira, the Red Hot Chili Peppers and U2. Bono – once he'd heard the chef had worked in Dublin – asked me to knock up a full Irish breakfast for forty members of his band's entourage one time.

I'd be below deck peeling potatoes or scrubbing mussels, but would always try to sneak up and peep at some celebrities. I was most star-struck by Sacha Baron Cohen, as Ali

G was huge at that time. I remember thinking he looked ever so serious, even a bit miserable. I guess money can't buy you happiness after all.

While the rich and famous were luxuriating, it was frantically busy below deck. The staff certainly partied after hours and everyone was young and hooking up with each other. Relationships were actually banned on many boats because of the problems it caused when couples fell out. But of course it was all going on.

There was access to any drink you could want because the boat was always fully stocked. Pink champagne, vodka, anything and everything. One time 150,000 euros' worth of champagne was ordered in, but the guests were Russian Orthodox and weren't drinking. There was an offer to reimburse them, but they just shrugged, 'let the staff drink it'. So we did. We even decadently filled up an entire Jacuzzi with the stuff and bathed in it, just because we could. Bonkers.

Blacking out after booze benders became normal. Then the paranoia would set in. *What did I say? Did I do anything stupid? Did I crack onto someone?*

I just couldn't deal with the hangovers. Feeling depressed and horribly anxious, I even emailed all the crew members saying I was an alcoholic, and that I was sorry and that I was leaving the boat the next day. I had this urge to tell people, it was a cry for help, but also I truly wanted to stop. It was hugely embarrassing.

I got pulled aside by my seniors, who were very kind and said they would support me. I was so mortified by the email and my general behaviour that I stayed sober for several months afterwards.

I fell off the wagon again though when we were on an idyllic beach in Sardinia. Everyone was cracking into the Aperol spritz. It looked so pretty.

Fuck this, I can't sit here drinking water. Everyone cheered as I took a sip. 'Oooh, he's back!' they laughed and clapped. It felt impossible not to drink in that environment.

Meanwhile, my dad back in Belgium had met a lovely young Irish lady, Grainne, and I flew back for 24 hours for the wedding. I was pleased he had found the happiness he really deserved (and am happy to report they now have two great sons of their own, Noah and Ruadh) but I can barely remember the wedding itself because I was so pissed. I passed out on the flight home dressed in my wedding suit, and even had to be carried off the plane by friends. Some of the yacht's guests had seen this happening, which was fairly shameful when I had to be serving them hours later.

But I wasn't alone in abusing alcohol, so it was easy to hide. There was a particularly wild night in Tahiti which saw a total of four staff members having to go to hospital with drink-related injuries. When the chief officer then put a booze ban on all staff, frankly, I was relieved.

★   ★   ★

After three years of excess in all senses, it was time to move on from the yacht-world madness, I thought. My final job in that industry was working for a much smaller boat in the Caribbean, cooking just for one elderly Canadian couple. There was a no-drinking policy on the boat, which was good for me. I'd long been googling 'am I an alcoholic?' knowing full well that I was.

While I was off the booze, I felt in better shape physically and mentally, and I'd started playing around with a digital camera of mine. Just for fun really, I made a simple video about how to cook the perfect steak, I edited it and uploaded it to YouTube, which was just in its first year. It got 100,000 views, which in those days was a lot.

There's something in this.

My business brain was ticking. I rang Sean, who was working in a bank by now, but I knew he was restless. How brilliant would it be to work with your best mate?

'We'll make these videos and put them on the internet, it's the future of cooking!' I told him excitedly. 'We're gonna be billionaires like Paul Allen!'

I moved back to Dublin, swept Sean up in my enthusiasm, and iFoods was born in 2007. The idea was to offer accessible and simple 'how to' videos: how to roast the perfect chicken, scramble the perfect egg, that kind of thing. To be fair, TikTok has proved there's a market for that sort of thing now. Back then we were a bit ahead of our time, and ahead of essential things like reliable broadband. But we didn't think it all through, we just assumed we'd make our millions from subscribers. That was the plan, anyway.

We both ploughed in 50,000 euros, along with a third partner, Peter, another chef. I can't stress enough how little I knew about business then. As a chef all my time had been spent in the kitchen; I wasn't media savvy or even very tech savvy. But I naively thought Sean could look after the business side of things, Peter would invest, and I'd be in front of the camera, like the new Jamie Oliver. I cringe about it all now.

The first one was a success. *This is easy!*

We were getting attention and Sean even got us a slot on *Dragons' Den*, which was a huge TV show at the time. We spent weeks preparing the pitch, and while we didn't get the investment backing from the Dragons, we got a lot of decent publicity. We had magazines interviewing us and iFoods had an app available on Apple.

But as newbies, we made every business mistake in the book, and blew all the cash in the process. The numbers dwindled, we felt under pressure, and the whole thing went tits up. What did I do? I drank wine heavily to combat the stress.

Sean blamed me, I blamed Sean. And we spectacularly fell out and stopped talking to each other for two years. It was a real fall from grace. We thought we were making it and we lost everything. I felt embarrassed that it hadn't worked.

By now Facebook, Twitter and blogging were all gaining popularity. I was 27 when I'd started chatting online to a girl in Brighton, Lauren Fisher, about the rise of social media. We could see it was going to be huge, and were both young and excited about this new tech era we were entering. Drunkenly (of course), I invited her to Dublin for the weekend. We hit it off, decided to go into business together and fell in love.

Between the pair of us we cobbled together ten grand and set up Simply Zesty in my spare bedroom, to keep overheads down. I'd learned a bit from my past entrepreneurial mistakes at least. Huge brands like Vodafone, Pepsi and Bank of Ireland all wanted a social media presence, but didn't know what to do, so Lauren and I 'consulted' for them, pitching ourselves as the experts in the space. Our expertise wasn't extraordinary by any means, but this area was new to everyone and we were enthusiastically, and with a reasonable amount of authority, getting stuck in.

The business blossomed, we soon had forty employees, and I was nominated for an Ernst & Young Entrepreneur of the Year award. It was a giddy time. We prioritised fun in the office: we had ping-pong tables, people drank together and bringing dogs into work was encouraged.

I was taken to New York for a business trip, where I went on such an epic bender I shamefully missed the flight home with the others, and found myself stuck in the Big Apple with no cash, no passport, no shoes and no friends.

Lauren wasn't impressed. In fact, as the business had grown our relationship had floundered. Working and living together was just too much pressure. Fearing Lauren would walk out like Mum had, I often pushed her away emotionally. It took therapy to be able to work that out. And of course my constant binge-drinking as well as the odd spot of gambling weren't helping. On top of that, a major addiction to Xanax had started.

If I've made any of this sound like some typical lad's binge-drinking years, please know this wasn't about high jinks or simply feeling a bit low. I found myself frequently in a very dark place indeed. Some days I was home alone drinking three bottles of wine along with Xanax. Sometimes I would puke from all the poisons I was putting into my body. Then once I'd been sick I would still drink more, or take cocaine to 'sober' me up and carry on drinking, drinking, drinking.

I found it impossible not to drink while watching sports. So when Manchester City's Sergio Aguero scored his famous goal against Queens Park Rangers in the 93rd minute to win the Premier League, I got totally shitfaced and managed to blow 3,000 euros (every last penny I had in the bank basically) in one afternoon making bets. Then realising how much I'd lost I carried on drinking to stop the fear setting in and to cheer myself up.

Whether I was celebrating or commiserating, out having fun or having a quiet night in, if I was going to a gig or watching any kind of football or rugby match – there was *always* an excuse to drink. Hangovers inevitably meant depression and anxiety to follow. I could hide in my room for several days at a time, miss meetings, blow out arrangements, let down friends. I'd spend absolutely any money I had in my pocket on my numerous vices, then be too broke to put petrol in the car to get to any meetings.

I really hadn't got my shit together at all.

In 2012 we were bought out by UTV, a public company, for 2 million euros. It was a lot of money. I bought a house in Dublin, and a Mercedes. I've never been a car person, but I somehow thought that was what you should do if you have the cash. It was stupid, but that was where I found myself.

It was around this time that I went and did something that would change my life forever.

I've never wanted kids. I guess I was terrified they'd turn out like me, and I'm not sure I'd want to inflict that on anyone. I also privately wondered, considering my appalling track record with relationships and women, whether I would ever actually be capable of holding down a proper marriage and doing the whole 2.4 kids thing that society seems to think is the norm. I've learned through hard-lived experience that I push away those people who love me and try and get close to me. I push them away emotionally for fear of getting hurt.

It might be that I've always been like this. And that's OK, I'm happy in my own company. But I've always suspected that I'm capable of giving love to animals. It's just less complicated, right?

I've always been drawn to dogs. I wouldn't necessarily coo over a baby (though I'm sure they're equally as cute). But I'd always be the person crossing the street to go and pat a four-legged friend. I'd actually dreamed of getting a dog for years. I felt like I'd be happy and could cope with anything if I had a dog. And the timing felt right.

So I took myself off to the ISPCA, which is like the RSPCA but in Ireland, to choose a rescue dog. I've always felt strongly that there were enough unwanted animals in the world and if I could provide a stable home for one, who would otherwise be unwanted, well, that to me was more important than buying a puppy.

A striking husky instantly caught my eye when I got to the rescue centre. They're glorious, stunning animals of course with their light coats and blue eyes. But the ISPCA guy (wisely in hindsight) explained that there was a dog he wanted to show me that he thought would be just perfect for a first-time dog owner, and led me to one in the kennels called Snoop.

Though far less remarkable-looking than the husky, Snoop was a black labrador cross-breed, with short sleek hair and a white chest and snout. They said he was two to three, but I think he was probably a bit younger than that.

Anyway, Snoop looked up at me with these huge, slightly sad brown eyes that seemed to beg 'Take me home, Niall' and honestly, he didn't need to really persuade me very hard. I crouched down to greet him and was delighted when he confidently came up to give me a good sniff. He had a stout body and held his head high like a nobleman. I took his big paddy paw in my hand and shook it a little. 'How do you do, Snoop?' I grinned.

And the uncomplicated buzz I experienced when he seemed to enjoy my attention on him lit up my soul. I felt something that I wasn't really used to without the use of drugs or alcohol – I felt happiness.

I fell in love with Snoop immediately. I didn't need to see any other dogs to make my decision, and no, I assured the ISPCA man, thank you very much but I didn't need any time to mull it over. I just knew in my heart that right here in this rescue centre, this was my dog. We instantly belonged to one another and were meant to be together. *Niall and Snoop. Snoop and Niall.* I wouldn't change his name; I wanted every single part of him exactly as he was.

I signed all the necessary paperwork the centre needed, gladly paid the fee, and I walked out of that centre on cloud nine. A stupidly proud dog owner leading my new best friend, tail wagging happily, along with me. Hand on heart, getting Snoop was the best decision I'd made in my life up to that point.

I put him in the car, feeling like we were already a team, Snoop and me. I couldn't wait to get him home and show him all the new stuff I'd bought: a bed, ball, food bowls. And he wouldn't leave my side, not because he was demanding or clingy at all. He was just happiest being my little shadow. That's how people described him, but no one remotely minded as he was so well-behaved, polite and unassuming.

He came to the office with me, he'd join me in meetings, he'd even come on dates with me. He'd encourage me to exercise, I'd take him on cycle rides with me, and we'd clock up one 10k run after another around the city's parks.

He was like another limb, an adorable, fluffy loyal one. If Snoop was with me, he'd be happy. He didn't look for anything or anyone else; being by my side made him walk tall and proud. I know that sounds incredibly egotistical of me, but some dogs are just like that with their owners. They're the only animals I know who love their human owners more than they even love themselves.

So as long as Snoop had food, water, a warm bed and me close by, he was perfectly content. He was the easiest dog in the world and became my absolute rock that I couldn't be without.

★   ★   ★

For a while, my life improved. Snoop helped my mental health, and I'd made up with Sean finally by this time. Our not-speaking stage had hurt me more than I cared to admit. He's like the brother I never had growing up, so it was so good to have my mate again. We both admitted we'd made mistakes and were keen to patch up the friendship. To celebrate, I took him and some friends on huge partying weekends in Berlin and Amsterdam. Of course it was great fun and full of high japes as you would expect from a few young guys out having a great time. But I can't deny I paid the price after those benders.

It wasn't just like nursing a hangover after a big bingeing weekend. My alcohol and drug abuse had gone way too far. I was in a truly wretched state.

Where other people could pick themselves up and get on with work and normal life, I would shamefully keep going by myself. I would pathetically self-medicate with more alcohol and drugs in private. Shutting the door to everyone and taking MDMA by myself. The comedowns and anxiety were destroying my mental health.

Knowing I needed help, I saw a therapist and worked through some of the rejection issues that were leading to the addictive patterns. I also went on anti-depressants. I knew I had to change, impose some self-control and break the patterns of spiralling into darkness. Somehow I managed almost a year sober, and set up a new media and marketing business, Lovin' Dublin, blogging about restaurants I'd been to, and other things to do in the city. I was always brutally honest when reviewing the latest eating joints in town, and people seemed to appreciate there was no bullshit.

It took off massively, and over the next four years I gained franchises in four other cities too, including Manchester. I got loads of media attention and was asked to speak at public events about my work and life. If only they knew how much I was struggling inside. I stood up there in front of crowds pretending I was super confident, giving it the big one, but I had complete imposter syndrome beneath the bravado. I always felt a fraud, like I didn't deserve the success I'd stumbled upon.

But as the business grew, inevitably my anxieties did too, as did my drinking binges. It was always a pattern with me. I would do six months or so sober, feel like I'd got it under control. *I've got this now.* Then I would have a beer. I told myself if I stuck to beer, or only drank at weekends, nothing bad would happen. I came up with all sorts of 'drinking rules'. Many people who battle alcohol issues say the same thing. We try to impose moderation, but it's a highly addictive substance, and for many people it's hard not to let the rules dominate your thoughts, which means lapsing is likely, if not inevitable. You play constant mind games with yourself and it's exhausting, until you always find a reason to 'give in' to them.

For a couple of weeks, the 'rules' would work, but sure enough I'd be back to the binges and the terrifying blackouts after that. When you blackout it's literally because your pickled brain can't take any more new information in. So when you do sober up eventually, and realise you just can't remember what you did, or said, or how you got home, well, the paranoia is just amplified. It's impossible to think straight, you catastrophise everything you possibly can. Your brain beats you up and goes round and round and it's just horrific.

Despite these binges and the chaos in my head, I was somehow able to function at work and Lovin' Dublin was becoming pretty successful. But with these sorts of businesses you can grow a decent reputation and yet at the same time not be bringing in loads of profit, and I was quietly burning through the lump sum of cash I'd made from selling Simply Zesty.

Sure, I'd bought some nice things, like the home and car, but I'd also be pissing plenty away on drinking nights, picking up bar tabs and gambling. Gambling is stupid anyway, but gambling when you're drunk is for the biggest idiots of all.

My bank balance was rapidly depleting, but to the outsider I was flying high. I felt embarrassed to admit the money had been trickling away. I had to put on the front of a successful entrepreneur, able to buy nice things and generously pay for meals for friends or work colleagues, when to tell you the truth, after a few years I was scrabbling around to raise 5 euros to buy a sandwich for lunch or a packet of fags, or even to put enough petrol in my car to drive it anywhere.

There were franchises now set up in Dubai and Manchester, and I decided to move to Manchester to get it off the ground for a year. I thought it would help to really immerse myself there and focus on work.

But my God, it was a miserable time for me. I had managed to be sober for a year (*well done, Niall!*), but when I suffered a terrible bout of truly debilitating depression I felt unbelievably frustrated. It felt unfair. I'd done everything by the book to stay healthy, I hadn't drunk, I was eating well, I'd gone for regular runs around Manchester's parks and suburbs, and cycled on long routes with Snoop running next to me, trying to battle my dark moods hoping endorphins from exercising would kick in.

It felt like me and Snoop had run 10,000 miles together during that time in Manchester. I knew that the exercise might help my mood, but there was a selfish element too, I must admit. I thought if I could tire out poor Snoop during the day, he could be all calm for me later in the night if I felt despairing – which I so frequently did.

On the days when I just couldn't run or walk – when I wasn't mentally or physically well enough even to just put one foot in front of the other – Snoop, bless him, was equally happy and understanding about that. Together we would look at the trees, I would try to breathe deeply and fully into my lungs, and try to dampen down the debilitating anxiety.

Yet there were days too when I just couldn't get out of bed. I couldn't see anyone, I couldn't face going to the shops or cooking food. A message popping up on my phone, especially anything work related, could send my anxiety sky high. I'd worry about whether I had done something wrong or upset someone. I couldn't even lose myself in a book for distraction; reading in bed was beyond me, I'd just want to put my head under the covers and cry. Every tiny thing that most people deal with on a daily or even hourly basis felt to me like a huge challenge, a mountain to climb.

Of course I would always force myself to take Snoop out to do his business, and to make sure he had food and water, but he somehow always knew and was understanding if that was all I could manage to do that day.

And Snoop would just lie loyally beside me, quiet as a mouse, curling into me and providing warmth and comfort. He'd do this time and time again; he knew I needed him and in those days in that cold, lonely apartment he was eternally patient with me and my moods, waiting with me until they eventually passed.

Dogs are so intuitive. In the same way that some clever dogs can be trained to sniff out bombs for the police or army, and some life-saving dogs can even be trained to sniff out cancers in humans before they can be otherwise detected, I always felt that Snoop could read exactly how I was feeling and how bad the depression was, and be there to soothe and comfort me.

There were times I felt like I couldn't be with anyone else, but I could always be with Snoop. By him just doing nothing other than being there for me, it was enough. A gentle prod with his nose, a look from his quizzical yet loving eyes. I knew that he loved me.

But there was still something missing in my life. *Why can't I love myself? I just want to feel normal. Why can't I just be normal?*

The Manchester weather was getting me down too. And people would say the weather in Ireland was bad. I was walking over some icy puddles one particularly shitty evening and … crunch! … my foot went straight through the ice and into the muddy water.

For fuck's sake.

A puddle sounds so ridiculous, and small, but it was the final straw.

I hated my life. I hated the weather in Manchester. I hated the business. I wanted out of the whole thing. I wanted to live somewhere hot with Snoop. Show him the sunshine.

I'm moving to Thailand.

And guess what? That's exactly what I did.

FOUR

THAILAND CALLING

While it had always been a long-held dream and distant ambition to escape the dreary rain and live in a tropical paradise, I didn't always know that the place calling me would be Thailand. Like many of my other decisions in life, it was instinct that brought me here. But I wasn't just closing my eyes and sticking a pin in a map.

I'd first been to Thailand for a sunshine break at the end of 2015. It was the perfect antidote to the winter; I've never been a fan of Christmas and it was a great excuse to miss the party season when I was on a non-drinking spell. I stayed for a couple of weeks and I fell in love with the place. The warm sands, the food, the laid-back atmosphere, the infectiously smiley locals. I felt at peace here. I came home genuinely feeling healthy for once. I returned the following year and stayed for a whole month.

I love the fact that there are no rules. No traffic wardens, no speed cameras. This is not a nanny state. People do what they want. There are many stereotypes of Thailand and while some of them still play a part in the lifestyle here, there are many more benefits to living out here.

There's so much to do. If you want to do yoga and eat at beautiful vegan restaurants, you can. If you want to go surfing or jungle trekking, you can do both. It had it all here, from the lively nightclubs to the relaxed beach life. I loved the fact people lived here with no judgement. There was no pressure to live in big houses and drive fancy cars. Life just seemed simpler.

I started thinking, *Why couldn't I just move to Thailand permanently?* There was nothing holding me back, I realised. I really wanted to do it. I needed a change. I was done with the UK, burned out and unhappy. The business was going well, starting to take off, but I'd lost interest. My heart wasn't in it.

But I couldn't just drop everything and run. The first thing I needed to do was sort out Lovin' Dublin. I rang the main investor in the business, Emmet O'Neill.

'Look, I just want out,' I explained. 'I'm sorry but I've had enough.'

When he realised I was serious and wasn't demanding loads of cash he happily agreed. Selling advertising in social media businesses takes a while before you see any cash. So he wouldn't have to pay that much to end up with a business that would potentially earn well.

We'd recently had somebody interested in buying the business and had turned them down because it wasn't for that much money. Emmet said yes, and the outline of the deal was wrapped up in just ten minutes. It was a situation that worked out quite well for everybody. And it meant I was free.

After clearing some debts I had, I knew I wouldn't be able to retire for life, but whatever was left over would be enough to live comfortably in Thailand until I could work out what I really wanted to do.

The first person I rang to tell them the news was Sarah, one of the website's writers. We'd become close friends from working together and I wanted to share my plans with her. She was surprised by the sudden decision, but also excited for me. There had always been a slight flirty attraction between us. She was a ridiculously smart and witty brunette, with a dry sense of humour. We really got on. I was older than her, aged 39 by now, and she was only 25. But we had fun and once I'd left Lovin' Dublin we became a couple that same week.

I was totally in love with her, to tell the truth. I told her about my plans to go to Thailand and travel.

'I'll come with you,' she said. It was quite a whirlwind romance and we were both swept along with it.

There were plans to put in place, practicalities that had to be finalised with work, friends' weddings to attend, and Snoop had to be taken care of by friends and family. It was the first time I'd have not been within a two-metre radius of Snoop since I'd welcomed him into my life. That worried me a bit, I have to admit. But I had good friends who look after dogs so I knew he would be well taken care of.

All in all it took five months to get ready for travelling. We flew to Thailand then travelled to other incredible parts of South East Asia, like Vietnam and Cambodia. We had a blast seeing this part of the world together, it was a free and easy time in my life.

Once we arrived in Thailand in December 2018 however, where I'd always planned to settle, the relationship problems began to set in. I had come home briefly to collect Snoop. I couldn't wait for him to explore and feel settled in our forever home of Thailand, and I was out there alone with him for the first month, while Sarah had things to tie up back home after our travels. But as soon as Sarah arrived to live with us, the relationship started falling apart. It was one thing dreaming of a future life together, but it turned out it was another thing actually living it together in a foreign country. The honeymoon period had ended and the realities … well, they just weren't quite as rosy.

She didn't like the place I'd picked to rent, a two-bedroom house with a small pool out the back, and she couldn't settle. I realised I'd been dreaming about living in Thailand with Snoop, on the beautiful island of Koh Samui where I'd loved visiting before, for so many months. But it was my dream all along. It hadn't really been hers, and I hadn't really factored her into the big picture, if I'm honest. It was easy to be in love when I'd just sold the business and wanted to travel the world. It had been so carefree and easy going. But now I wanted to make Thailand my forever home – for Snoop and me. And truthfully I wasn't sure where Sarah fitted in.

We bumbled along for a bit and started building a travel business together focusing on recommendations and guides for travel around the world, which was fairly successful, but in March 2020, when Covid reared its ugly head, turning the world upside down, Sarah and I were suddenly stuck together 24/7. There was no point writing about travel when no one was allowed to go anywhere. And Thailand had shut its borders and there was no chance of her getting a flight back to Dublin, or indeed anywhere else.

Like many other panicking couples across the globe, we stockpiled as much booze as we physically could and gritted our teeth through the pandemic, locked down together with Snoop. It's fair to say it wasn't harmonious.

There were lots of tense times and rows. My drinking had got way out of hand again with little else to do all day, and I remember Sarah furiously pouring wine down the sink one time and yelling that I had to stop and that drink was killing me. Of course I knew in my heart she was absolutely right, and yet all I could think of in my selfish, addict way, was that I just wanted her to leave so I could drink in peace.

In all honesty, it was a relief for us both when travel restrictions were lifted and she was finally able to leave Thailand in December 2020.

* * *

After Sarah left, I wasn't in a happy place. But there were always people to drink with, so I'd tell myself it would 'cheer me up' and do me good to go for a drink. An alcoholic always has an excuse to hand, whatever the occasion. Koh Samui is full of ex-pats escaping life and there's always someone propping up a bar. It's an easy place to waste your life away in the sunshine. No one questions you if you're drinking beers in the morning. It's always someone's holiday here.

The depression was terrible at this time. I'd often have tears running down my face for no apparent reason. I started buying Valium frequently: it's so easy to get out here, you can just walk into the chemists and get it over the counter.

In hindsight, I was in complete mental breakdown mode, on self-destruct. I couldn't organise my own dinner even. For someone who was once so proud to create dishes and flavours, I didn't give a shit. I had no instinct to look after myself and I stopped eating properly. I made sure my beloved Snoop was fed, but feeding myself? I just didn't care about nurturing my body. Alcohol was the only thing on my mind.

I'd wake up unbelievably anxious, holding my heart and feeling it pound away furiously in my ribcage. I was relying on Valium to function through the anxiety, and I was relying on it to put me back to sleep if I could. I'd look at my phone for two hours in the middle of the night – the football scores, the news back home, social media. Anything to distract me from the self-destructive thoughts and the mess in my head.

I started drinking in the middle of the night. If I woke up, a couple of glasses of red wine might help me back to sleep, I reasoned. It was always red by then, I'd stopped drinking white wine just because the extra hassle of having to keep it cool in the fridge was too much of an effort.

Any rules I'd previously imposed on myself about alcohol – about days, or times, or amounts – all went out the window. With Sarah gone I didn't care whether there were bottles by my bed or strewn across the living room. And you've guessed it, it was Snoop who was right by my side, who could not and would not give up on me. He was just always there, eyes looking wide and a little concerned for me perhaps, cocking his head to one side quizzically, but never judging me, just remaining loyally by my side.

He's a quiet dog, reserved and a real gentleman, that's what everyone says about Snoop. He's not super playful, or even super cute to other people I imagine. But he has always been there throughout all the lows, sitting by my feet when I was miserable. He can read my moods better than anyone. We are so weirdly in sync he even does this thing where he clicks his teeth when I'm depressed. I should really use it as a warning that a dark time is coming and I need to buckle in for the ride.

We are best buddies forever, me and Snoop, and at this point in my life it felt like he was all I had. And if I hadn't had my loving Snoop by my side I might have been in an even bigger mess, to be honest. He never judged me. He never gave up on me. Day after day, he sat patiently with me throughout these times. It seemed I was rubbish at relationships with women. Snoop was the only one who had put up with me.

With the alcohol, it didn't bother me when I had to keep going back to the same shop to buy more and more bottles from the same person. If they disapproved, I didn't care. I was beyond feeling shame. If I'd had the foresight when drunk to go to the 7/11 shop and buy enough booze for when I woke up, that would be a win, something to pat myself on the back about. In any 24-hour window my booze tally could be something like ten cans of beer, four bottles of wine, a bottle of Thai whiskey, five Valiums, plus forty-odd Camel Light cigarettes.

Lonely and desperate, I had embarrassing drunken meltdowns on Twitter, of all places. I shared some pictures of my apartment – strewn with empty wine and whiskey bottles, cans of beer and overfilled ashtrays, crisp packets and chocolate-bar wrappings – with desperately dramatic captions like 'This is what addiction looks like.' It was clearly a cry for help from a beaten, lonely and depressed man. Yet I refused to answer any of the worried calls from people who'd seen the posts and were trying to help me.

My parents and friends were all horrified and wanted to help, but I refused to communicate with them. And I knew they wouldn't be able to get on a plane to fly to Thailand with all the various Covid restrictions anyway. Sarah was frantically phoning me, worried what would happen next, offering to come back and help me. I even had therapists and professionals – strangers I didn't know from Adam – reaching out to me after seeing the manic posts online and begging me to get help. I'd be mortified by my Twitter outbursts as soon as I'd sobered up a bit and then try and play down things. But I really was in a sorry state.

FIVE

ROCK BOTTOM ... AND RECOVERY

When it comes to addiction issues, you might have heard the phrase 'rock bottom'. This is the part of an addict's 'journey', if you want to call it that, when they reach their absolute lowest ebb.

In fact, some rehabilitation places say that you haven't reached your rock bottom until you are, quite literally, dying. When your body has given up the will to live and when even your loyal, dutiful internal organs – thanks to months, years or decades of abuse – have finally called time on keeping you alive. They've had enough now. And the grim reaper is pounding on your door.

This was the state I found myself in when I reached my own rock bottom, on New Year's Eve 2020.

One booze binge and Valium cycle just merged messily into the next. I was sick of all the noise going round and round in my head. I was a failure for breaking up with Sarah, letting the drink and my constant drive to get absolutely off my head destroy the relationship. I put booze and drugs and my own selfish needs ahead of hers. Ahead of everything.

The humiliating fool I made of myself on Twitter, saying what a mess I was in – of course I was, but I was mentally torturing myself with having told the entire world about my fuck-ups. I couldn't stop crying half the time. I'd be sitting in a bar, alone, with tears streaming down my face. People were encouraging me to come out. Join us! Have fun! It's Christmas! But I was in no state to socialise, I was sick in the head. I just wanted to drink at home. Pass out. Then drink again.

People back home were worried, I knew that. They urged me to come and see them, the family in Northern Ireland or the friends back in Dublin. But because it was still during Covid, travelling was too problematic. I couldn't possibly have got my muddled mind organised enough to think about passports and visas.

In the end, I agreed to spend time with some local friends here in Thailand. Morritz, a fellow ex-pat was having a pleasant, civilised Christmas dinner at his villa on Christmas Eve (lots of my friends were European and that's the tradition there). They were friends I'd made from playing football mainly and their respective partners.

I drove over to their house feeling queasy, sick and anxious about even the idea of being in company. So I had a couple of beers to calm me down before I even left my apartment. Then, I got a Coke bottle and emptied it of fizzy pop all but for a couple of inches at the bottom. I topped up the rest of the bottle with Thai whiskey. This was because I knew there would be a part of the afternoon where people would be outside and enjoying the day and festivities and booze wouldn't be opened until later. I knew I couldn't cope during that small window without a bit of help. So while the friends happily chatted away, I was necking my 'special drink'.

I got through the first hour or something on that whiskey. Then, luckily, people started pouring gin and tonics and of course I got stuck in hard, necking those before the start of the meal.

Naturally, I got too drunk too quickly because of the secret whiskey. *Uh-oh*. I knew I was in trouble being in such a state even before the starters had been served. A couple of people were looking at me in a strange way while exchanging looks. It made my paranoia worse. Jesus, I was drunk. And very conscious of it. I just couldn't keep it together at all among all these normal, happy, successful people having a civilised get-together.

I was trying to make conversation with them. But tears began flowing, as they so often did for no apparent reason. I was stumbling, slurring and dropping things. I was *so* hammered. All over the place. I got up out of my seat to go to the loo and fell over and smacked my face. I didn't do any damage, thank God, just hit the ground in a heap.

People could tell it wasn't funny. No one laughed. They jumped up to help with concern etched on their faces.

'Jesus, we need to get you home,' I recall someone saying. Morritz walked me to a taxi. He's such a nice guy. It would never have occurred to him that I would spend all day drinking myself stupid. I'm sure my level of depravity wouldn't have crossed his innocent mind.

Even in that sorry state, I still managed to get the cab to stop at the 7/11 to pick up more booze, because I knew if I didn't pass out that night I would be craving it as soon as I woke in a few hours.

I'm patchy about what happened next. I'm guessing I would have gone to sleep, perhaps woken and drunk some more wine. Felt more anxious, then popped more Valium. I'd be delighted with myself for getting the booze in first. *You're so fucking smart, Niall.* Surrounded by a large glass of wine, whiskey, bottles of beer and overflowing ashtrays. *Well done, me.* I'd always take enough Valium until I believed I wasn't about to die.

The aim was just to drink until oblivion arrived as a merciful escape. I don't think I wanted to actually end my life, or anything like that, but it was like I was trying to drink myself to death. I felt that if I drank enough I just wouldn't wake up tomorrow, and that was OK. That'll be a better place.

I kept the bender going for the next five or six days and then one night, convinced I was dying but too frightened to die alone and paralysed with fear and anxiety, I called and begged Morritz to come and take me to a private hospital. Even in that state I knew there was no point clog-ging up the general hospital for other people. I had cash in the bank and would have handed anything over just for them to let me in and give me some meds to help.

The staff were dubious about taking me in initially. They looked at me suspiciously and spoke in hushed tones. There was a suggestion I should wait until the alcohol dependency unit opened the following week. I think my Thailand tan perhaps made me look healthier than I was. But there was no denying I was a sobbing, shaking, stink-ing mess.

'This man needs urgent help – now!' insisted Morritz. I was grateful for his clear, Germanic authority in those moments.

Sure enough they found me a bed in a room in the ICU. I was hooked up to all sorts of monitors and then a nurse came in wielding the largest needle I'd ever seen and gave me a shot of a powerful sedative in my leg. I was given a cocktail of pills to help with the alcohol withdrawal. Morritz offered to stay with me, but I wouldn't hear of it. It was New Year's Eve, he should be having fun, I didn't want to drag him into this place. He promised me Snoop would be taken good care of in my absence, and then I had nothing else to do but get through whatever came next.

And I truly wouldn't have wished the next 48 hours on my worst enemy. Despite the sedatives I couldn't really sleep, and when I did I had hideous hallucinations about my beloved Snoop eating chocolate and being poisoned. I knew he was being taken good care of, by dog-loving friends, but the images were so vivid.

I had complete paranoia. Anytime I heard a noise I thought it was the police coming to arrest me for the Valium I'd bought. Although it's freely available to buy over the counter in Thailand, I wasn't sure whether it was one hundred per cent legal. Anything I could possibly fret about, and magnify, I did.

Against the backdrop of fireworks banging and crackling outside, and party-goers cheering and laughing as they merrily welcomed in the New Year, I lay shivering and shaking in my thin hospital gown, hooked up to drips and monitors. I shut my eyes to the chinks of outside life which I could glimpse from my bed. And wondered whether I would even make it.

I hadn't been in any fit state to pack a phone charger for the hospital (or even any spare boxers), and with the escape of sleep just not happening, all I had to do was listen to the *beep, beep, beep* of my heart monitor and sound of the clock hands slowly *tick, tick, ticking*. Just willing the time on until I could get my next injection of sedative. I was still on a drip and being urged to drink water. I could barely manage a thimbleful but I kept going. I nibbled on some melon, a mouthful of yoghurt, but eating was almost impossible. Even a trip to the loo seemed like running a marathon, the poor nurses would have to come and unhook me from the drips, and I'd have to gear myself up for half an hour to attempt the bathroom.

When it was clear I was too wobbly to take a shower alone, the nurses had to help wash me. I felt deeply ashamed standing there pathetically naked, it can't have been nice for them having to wash some stinky, shaking alcoholic. I shut my eyes and wanted to die of shame.

Finally, after 48 hours in ICU, I was deemed well enough to be put in a room off a main ward. Lying in bed all those long hours certainly offered plenty of thinking time about my life. Aside from my family, loved ones and Snoop, nothing else mattered to me. Being a chef, building and selling businesses, media appearances, awards – all stuff I'd thought was important and that I'd spent so long working towards. When push came to shove, those things meant fuck-all to me.

I realised I wasn't ready to die. I wanted to live. I had to make my time count. Whether or not I deserved it, I was being given a second chance, and I vowed I would do it differently next time …

I decided to take a year off after being in hospital. It was time to focus on myself and my rehabilitation in every sense of the word. Recovery was very slow though. After spending a quarter of a century of working all hours and drinking all hours, my brain was totally fried.

I felt certain I was truly done with alcohol for good. My ugly and long relationship with it was over and I wouldn't be dragged back in by temptation now. I went for long walks with Snoop, letting him sniff at flowers and follow my path as I ambled through the jungle. I savoured the sunsets and the sensation of sand between my bare toes. I read books and browsed the internet looking for answers about life from wiser people than me.

One of the things that really struck home was the famous 'Commencement' speech the late, great Steve Jobs made in 2005 at Stanford University, where he said, 'Remembering that I'll be dead soon is the most important tool I've ever encountered to help me make the big choices in life.'

It felt so spot-on to me. After staring death in the face myself, I knew that whatever I did next, I had to do with all my heart and soul. I'd wasted so many years.

I knew one day I would be back in a hospital bed truly breathing my final breaths, and that was OK. That's life. The only important thing was making whatever time I had left actually count.

But it wasn't like I knew overnight what form my making a difference might take. It took a whole year of recovery – from lying in that hospital bed, watching those minutes tick by painfully slowly until I could get my next sedative – to map out a mission and find my life's vocation. I was weak and needed to slowly build up my physical and mental strength. For anyone who is battling addiction recovery, I would urge them to take it one minute, then one hour, and then one day at a time. If you've spent decades abusing your body and mentally beating yourself up, well, you can't expect to bounce back in a week.

I know I am incredibly privileged, because I had money in the bank to support myself, and living in Thailand is relatively cheap. I don't have a partner or children. It's just me and Snoop. I appreciate that a single, working parent battling an addiction does not have these luxuries.

I was able to shop for and cook good food for myself. I was able to commit to being healthy, going for runs, bike rides, swimming in the sea, having regular massages and treating my body with respect and love instead of abuse and shame. Well-meaning friends were kind and invited me to things like board-game nights where there would be no pressure to drink, but I honestly found it easier to just stop socialising for a good while. I never once relapsed into old habits, thank God. I know I never will. The ICU scare had been all too real.

On a day-to-day basis, unlike other times in my life where I have stayed sober for several months and once for a year, I knew that now I was truly done forever with drinking. For a long time I had to avoid certain triggers, like watching any kind of sporting match which I'd long associated with having a beer in my hand. Socialising with certain friendship groups, sitting in bars – I had to take them all out of the equation until I knew I was genuinely strong enough.

One of the things that most calmed me down during these months was going for long walks in the jungle. Breathing in the fresh air, looking at trees gently blowing in the warm winds, it all helped dampen the anxiety and clear my mind. It made me feel alive and full of gratitude to still be here on this earth. That might sound annoyingly hippy-ish, but it's true. Koh Samui is such a special place, a tropical island full of beauty and wonder. And I was lucky enough to be living here.

I think about the silly things I used to waste money on and feel foolish now. I love the fact that my entire wardrobe here consists of ten pairs of shorts and ten t-shirts, all from the local markets, three pairs of flip-flops and boxer shorts. I've got two hoodies for the rainy season in November and December, and that's about it. That's all I need and all I want.

I knew I'd made the right decision to move here to live simply with Snoop, seeing him play in the sea and run on the sand alongside me. I finally felt free.

SIX

LUCKY ... THE LONER WHO STARTED IT ALL

Now that I was sober and had Snoop for company, I began taking more of an interest in dogs, and in particular strays. Thailand has millions of street dogs, there are tens of thousands on the island of Koh Samui alone, and unless you've been here, or seen some videos, it might be hard to imagine the scale, or picture them all wandering around.

You'll find dogs on most street corners, outside shops and around any areas where humans live. They'll normally stay on their own little patch, about a 100-metre radius, so it's easy to spot the same ones if you only stop ignoring them.

Whenever I saw a gorgeous dog I'd feel an extra spring in my step. I had my lovely, loyal buddy Snoop at home and couldn't be without him. But the street dogs literally lit me up from inside and made me feel alive. I'd be crossing the road or parking up my scooter just to say hello. A little pat, some tummy rubs, a waggy tail – the best therapy in the world. My phone was always full of pictures, and every second one would be of a puppy.

I wasn't sure how many of them even survived. It could be heartbreaking to see some of the states they were in. Ridden with fleas and worms, infected with ticks, frequently they seemed injured, hobbling. Usually by either a whack from a car, fighting with each other over scarce food, or even from snake attacks.

And yet the will to live and their spirits were amazingly unbroken, despite their tough lives. A dog might limp up to me with a horrible injury, and yet still be able to look at me, wide eyed and curious, with love and trust, and muster a tail wag somehow.

Most of them formed small packs, sticking together for company as well as some protection from other dogs, and possibly bad humans. All are strays with no owners: some will have been abandoned because they got sick and people couldn't afford vet fees, others will have been born and bred on the streets, never wanted by anyone.

For the dogs in the jungle, life is even harder. Some get kicked out of their packs and will live near some migrant workers' shacks where they might get some scraps of food from humans, and be close to a stream for water. It's not that the locals are cruel, but most people here don't have much money to feed themselves, never mind the dogs. They're just accepted as being there, and left to get on with it.

I had no great plan originally, but seeing the dogs were often frail and generally always starving, I started buying some bags of dried food to feed them. A big bag of kibble (dried dog food) from the shop costs 500 baht (about 15 euros) and I would start laying it out, in piles on the ground, or on an old coconut shell or palm leaf if I saw one, and they would gratefully lap it up. It was like they couldn't believe their luck being offered food that they didn't have to scavenge for.

After just a couple of days of doing this I realised the dogs were waiting for me as soon as they heard the bike engine. 'Hey little fellas,' I'd grin, seeing them jump up and obviously glad to see me. Their welcomes were so warm and unconditional. I realised how awful it would be if I didn't appear the next day, if I broke the routine and they were left waiting for me. I imagined their little downcast faces, pawing at the mud. I didn't want to let them down.

I kept buying more kibble for them, and after a week it dawned on me I was fully committed to these stray dogs now – and what's more I was genuinely more than happy to feel helpful and wanted. After years of feeling I was a waste of space, I guess it was pathetically gratifying.

At first, it was only taking me about an hour a day and it was lots of fun, so simple and yet incredibly rewarding. For the first time in a while I felt real joy while in their uncomplicated company, and then real contentment afterwards. At least half of the dogs I noticed wanted affection and for me to sit with them and play just as much as they wanted the food I was bringing. Some were a little timid, but they soon warmed up.

Because of my relationship with Snoop and liking dogs, I always felt relaxed around them, and in turn they were relaxed around me. If you're nervous and uptight in their company, the dogs pick up on it and get tense and then bark, which I appreciate doesn't endear them to people. But that's just like humans in fairness. Ninety-nine per cent of them are amazing, but there's always the odd nutter in there ...

The kibble wasn't expensive, but I worked out that buying it in bulk, from a wholesale store rather than the local shop, was far more cost effective. It meant more hungry canine mouths could go to sleep with food in their little furry bellies. So I started adding more dogs to my round, there was no point lugging leftover kibble back home with me, and it was so easy to find hungry dogs grateful for the food and attention. The hardest thing at that stage was knowing that others were hungry and lonely as well, and having to fight the real temptation to take some of the more frail ones home with me each day.

There was one dog in particular, a lithe, graceful girl with cream fur and alert, pointy ears, who particularly tugged at my heartstrings. I'd started playing football every week with some local friends. It was good to get some exercise with the guys, try and keep myself on track physically and mentally, get the endorphins pumping and blow off some cobwebs.

I was just driving home on my bike, feeling quite nicely knackered after one of our kickabouts, when I first spotted her.

She was on the side of the track looking slightly frail, like her legs were slightly long for her body, though she wasn't a young puppy. She had bad skin, with fresh sores, older scars and bald patches in places. She'd clearly been in a fair few scraps with something bigger than her. But despite that, when I pulled my bike over to have a better look at her she seemed genuinely delighted I was stopping to say hello. Her tail wagged eagerly, her mouth relaxed and her bright eyes were filled with curiosity.

While all the other dogs I'd come across needed food, and she was certainly starving and underweight, it was clear she needed a little more help than just some kibble to get back on her feet. She held my gaze inquisitively, almost disconcertingly for a dog, like she could see into your soul. I returned for the next couple of days, intrigued by her. She had a sort of 'otherness' quality about her, a self-contained separateness from the pack.

Each time I came she instantly devoured any food I offered, but it always seemed to be love or affection that she was the most hungry for, with her slightly pleading expression. She craved attention and strokes before she made a beeline for the kibble. I also sadly realised that she seemed to be shunned by all the other dogs, or they'd pick on her, throwing a growl or a bark her way, and she was by nature a real loner. It was something I could certainly relate to, though it seemed more unusual in canines.

Living totally alone in the jungle without a pack for protection or companionship seemed to be her choice though. Yet when she did come to find me she clearly loved humans and had such a warm and responsive nature. I wish I could have known more of her back story, or be able to read it in her intelligent black eyes. All I could think to do at first was to try and get her to bulk up a bit, as she was worryingly thin and you could see all her bones. But fattening her up wasn't easy as she wouldn't come every day to find me.

As well as being a loner, she was somewhat elusive. I soon found myself automatically scanning Koh Samui's jungle paths, bushes and greenery for sight of her light-coloured fur and proud independent figure. When I couldn't seem to find her for four days in a row, I worried. Had something happened to her? Was that the last I'd seen of her? I felt a fool for getting so attached to a roaming random dog. I'd looked in all her regular haunts and was just feeling dejected, packing up for the day to head home back to Snoop, when she came bounding around the corner of a shack, like a little golden vision, an angel.

My favourite girl was back! Honestly, I think my heart did a little skip with joy, I was that pleased to see her. I know I wasn't really supposed to have favourites, but she'd quickly become mine. I felt stupidly touched because she seemed just as overjoyed to see me as I felt to be reunited with her. I checked out the state of her physique as I gave her the last of the bag of kibble I'd been saving, just in case she turned up.

I spotted she had a few injuries from whatever she'd been up to. But despite being hungry and sore she still wanted to play as she always did. I threw a piece of kibble into the air and she pounced up to snatch it cleverly in her mouth. She rolled on her back with her tongue lolling out indicating her belly needed a rub, please. I laughed and made a huge fuss of her. Then having to say goodbye at the end of that day was surprisingly hard.

'I'll be back tomorrow,' I promised her. 'You'll come back and see me won't you, lovely girl?'

I hoped she'd be back. I kept to my word and visited every day. Over the next ten days she came for five of them. Determined to boost her weight, and not knowing when she would next appear, I always gave her especially generous helpings of food, and I was happy to note she was at least starting to look less painfully thin.

There are so many dogs out here in Koh Samui that it's hard to name them all, but I'd posted some of her pictures and videos on my Twitter and Instagram accounts, and someone called Ivor on Twitter suggested the name Lucky … it fitted her perfectly. She was happy-go-lucky by nature, and we were both so lucky to have met each other.

I was desperate to help her more, I knew just feeding her alone was only a short-term measure. But I was no expert when it came to animals, and I genuinely didn't know what was the best thing to do. My mind, always a busy place, started whirling with ideas. I knew I couldn't just take in every poor dog I saw; there were twenty others like Lucky in a similar uncared-for state. I'd clearly bonded with her, but I had to be strict with myself and come up with a bigger, better and more practical solution to help more of them.

I couldn't scoop her up and take her with me. I didn't think Snoop would have minded, he's Mr Laidback. But Lucky would never be at ease living in a normal human house, that was obvious from the start. She was a creature used to doing her own thing and going her own way in life. That's how street dogs have existed here for decades, they're not like domesticated pets we have at home. They're tougher because they've had to fend for themselves for so long. They're quite hardy as they haven't ever relied on humans. They're used to their freedom, their territories; to put them in a house and expect them to be happy with a daily walk like a pet would probably be distressing to many of these dogs. It would go against their natural instinct.

It might not make any sense to you and me, but the streets and jungle is like their home, and they'd choose that over a comfy bed in a house probably, because it's what they know. They have their own routines and sources of food and water and they're often happiest in their natural environments.

So I couldn't just take Lucky home and expect her to live peacefully with me. But I wanted to try and find her a nice home of some sort out here in the jungle. Somewhere she would have some protection from the elements and other dangers. I decided that at least I could get her vaccinated against the most common and preventable illnesses, and I could get her minor injuries on her cream fur all fixed up. I could get her neutered at least, so she wouldn't have to deal with puppies, and I'd buy her a collar with a tag. A sign to her, and everyone else, that this was a dog someone actually gave a shit about.

It might all be a challenge, I had no idea what she'd make of it, but this girl was worth it and I knew it would help her in the long run to stay safe.

I'm not a particularly woo-woo person, who goes in for fate and all that. Not normally anyway. But I did genuinely feel like we'd met by serendipity, and this would be the start of a new chapter for her. Kneeling to her level I held out my hand, and quick learner that she was, she offered me her paw in return, and cocked her head inquisitively. I felt like we were making a deal together. As if she were saying, 'Pleased to get to know you Niall, let's do this together.' Perhaps this wouldn't just be a new chapter for her, but for me too.

I felt like I had a good plan in theory, but it took me the best part of a week to get hold of her, and actually start putting it into action. I took myself off to a local pet store and bought Lucky a collar, a brightly coloured orange and yellow one, that would make her easier to find I thought. It had a little bell on it too, so I could hear her coming.

First I gently trained her to walk on the lead just up and down a stretch of jungle road. That was clearly very new to her, but bless her she seemed willing to give it a try, looking at me for approval. 'Good girl, Lucky,' I reassured her. And she didn't object at all when I fastened her collar around her neck.

I didn't fancy my chances of safely transporting her on my moped though, so I asked a friend to borrow a car, and Lucky allowed herself to be coaxed into the back of the vehicle. She seemed nervous at first, she was quivering slightly, but she seemed to sense I was trying to help her and trusted that I wasn't the enemy. I knew there wasn't any rabies on the island of Koh Samui, so that wasn't so much of a fear, but I was a little worried I'd get fleas or ticks from her. I just didn't really know what to expect and what might happen when trying to take a wild street dog to the vet.

Lucky was definitely glad to get out of the car when we reached the veterinary surgery. The vet no doubt was inwardly rolling her eyes and thinking, *Who the hell is this mad white man bringing in a street dog to me?* But her English and my basic Thai didn't exactly lend itself to a full discussion of the issue.

It wasn't the first time the vet had seen a street dog in the surgery. There were charities already working with street dogs long before I came along, and sometimes ex-pats or foreigners on holiday here would take pity on injured animals and bring them in, too. At the end of the day, the vet's job was to help animals, and here was a dog who needed some assistance, and here I was happy to pay for the treatment.

The vet took blood tests and gave Lucky a thorough examination. The dog, she guessed, was between one and two years old. You can tell a dog's age by looking at their teeth, she explained. They're still quite white in the first couple of years, and older dogs can have more smelly breath from bad diets. Lucky had no parasites, which is rare for street dogs and something positive at least. Perhaps it was because she wasn't mingling with other dogs, I wondered? An X-ray also showed that Lucky had already been spayed. Wherever she had come from in the past, this was good news. Lucky wouldn't have to try and cope with puppies on top of her own survival.

Yet as I suspected, there was bad news in store too. There was a bunch of stuff wrong with my girl. Her lymph nodes were swollen, which is usually a sign of bigger problems, she had worms, skin issues, a liver problem and irregular blood levels.

'Oh Lucky,' I said, giving her big pointy ears an affectionate stroke.

She nuzzled into my arm, as if to say, 'Thank you for taking care of me, Niall.'

It blew my mind that she could have so much physically wrong with her and yet still have such great energy, spirit and verve. She really was a very special dog. It felt fantastic to be helping her.

The vet was able to give her four sets of medicine which would help all of her issues. I knew I had to somehow make sure she got them all. I wanted Lucky better and living the life she deserved, now that I'd been able to get her seen and diagnosed.

After the trip to the vet's, I decided to take Lucky back to my apartment and was able to give her a good wash down with the hose and the special dog shampoo I'd bought her. Snoop came and had a friendly enough nosey at this strange skinny newcomer in his home, but he wasn't especially interested. He looked up at me, seemed to shrug 'whatever' and sloped back off to his bed unfazed.

He's such a gentleman though, he'd never be remotely aggressive or territorial. I was all excited seeing Lucky's fur completely changing colour as the grime washed away down the plughole. She was several shades lighter when actually clean. Her coat gleamed now. 'Take a look at this, Snoop!' I said, rubbing her dry with an old towel.

Lucky had let me clean her, but she refused to really

settle at my apartment. As trusting and friendly as she was with me, the indoors unnerved her. At heart she was a street dog through and through.

We played for a while, but she became restless and unrelaxed. She started sniffing and scratching to get out at the door, and was clearly very eager to get back to her own familiar patch in the jungle among the trees, streams and mud tracks. The freedom to roam where she pleased. The walls and smooth floors of my place were all alien to her paws. The smells were different. There were no birds to be heard.

'It's OK, Lucky, I'll take you back,' I told her. 'But you have to promise me you'll come back for food and your medicines for the rest of the month, OK?'

I like to think she understood me and even gave me a little nod that she would.

I drove her home and watched her skip back into the jungle, sniffing the trees as she trotted off.

'I'll see you tomorrow then Lucky!' I called after her.

Knowing Lucky was happily back in her safe place that evening, with a belly full of food and lots of medicine, made me happy that I'd achieved something that day.

She had been gentle, patient and willing to learn and share her first-time experiences with me – she'd been on a lead, travelled in a car and visited the vet's – even though she was clearly petrified. We'd both been well outside our comfort zones that day, but we were in this together now.

I don't have a tail myself to wag, but I walked a little taller that night. I'd got some sense of purpose. Lucky still had a long way to go of course, but I couldn't wait to find her again the next morning and see how her full recovery to health would unfold over the coming month. With that unbreakable spirit she really deserved this second chance in life.

I might have had Lucky sorted out in the short to medium term, but helping her in the small ways I had done was only the first baby step in what I realised should become a bigger mission. There were so many dogs like Lucky. How could I do good by as many of them as possible?

I felt like I had the capacity and ability to help them. I just wasn't sure how. My background was all in cooking and then setting up businesses in social media. I wasn't shy of hard work, and I knew how to grow a successful business, but trying to improve the lives of street dogs? That was entirely different.

So far I'd been acting instinctively by feeding the dogs and then getting Lucky to the vet, but I'd been cobbling it together, making it up as I went along. I knew nothing about veterinary care, sterilising dogs en masse, or other elements I knew would be needed. I suspected there were many more things I hadn't even thought of yet.

The biggest concern was that Lucky was only one dog out of at least fifty I could have picked to do the same for.

She was truly 'lucky' in that respect, as there are many others out there who will have similar or worse issues. Street dogs are used to fending for themselves, but not having access to health care when they're sick is the crucial difference between pets and those living in the wild.

They're forced to battle on and learn to live with disease or illnesses that could well be treated. But the less health care they get the sicker they become and they start looking even less appealing to locals. People see them as 'manky' and scare them away or are fearful of catching something horrible, but many illnesses could be easily prevented or treated.

Switching on the table lamp at my desk, with Snoop snoozing away by my feet, oblivious to my newly found purpose, I turned on my laptop and stared at the sums in front of me.

Lucky's vet visit and medication came in at 4,500 baht (€120/$135). When you consider that a typical local salary can be between 10,000 and 12,000 baht per month, it's easy to see why many dogs here do not get the simple medical care they need.

I didn't mind doing this for a few. Living in Thailand was cheaper than at home, so I could string it out for a while. But that pot of cash wouldn't last forever. Covering the cost of feeding the dogs wasn't super expensive at 500 baht a day (€13/$15). I worked out I could feed twenty-five a day and look after a handful medically, but I really wanted to do so much more.

When I was buried in work before I lived in Thailand, I'd always airily imagined myself starting a charity in later years, when I had nothing left to do personally or professionally. But it had dawned on me then that just wasn't good enough. I needed to start helping, to start giving back something, *now*.

Long term I knew the strategy needed to be around neutering and health treatments rather than just food, because every day I could find a new pack of dogs. Just that week I'd pulled back some bushes and found six little big-eared beauties staring hopefully back at me. The feeding round could get bigger and bigger with more hungry mouths to feed. I envisioned my moped toppling under the weight of gigantic kibble sacks. When would it end?

With fire in my belly that I hadn't felt for years, I stayed up long into the night dreaming up my ludicrously ambitious aim – to help 10,000 dogs every month. If you were to ask me why I pulled out that particular target from my head, the truthful answer is, I am not really sure. I'd love to say there was some scientific, well thought-out reason for it, but there really wasn't. It just happened to be a big number that I could understand (like 10,000 daily steps or a 10k run) and one that although seemed terrifyingly daunting at that point, I still felt might be achievable, within the realms of possibility.

I pledged to try and look after that amount of dogs on a monthly basis. Giving them a better life, a better chance of being healthier, or even saving them from death or illness somehow.

I had no real clue how long it might take to reach this target. A year? A decade? Or even the rest of my life? But I vowed that getting there would become my North Star that would guide me from now on. It was like the year of recovery that I'd just come out of was getting me to the place where I needed to be, to be strong enough to take on something like this, a real project to do good.

I had to really consider what 'this' would involve, and came to the conclusion it would basically be by dedicating every waking moment to the mission for the rest of my life. I've always been an all or nothing person. Everything I would do would be tied back to how I could use my time to help more dogs, and get to that achievement of helping 10,000 every month.

I knew I wanted to be hands-on with the dogs and carry on caring for them every day, but I also thought that with my background in social media businesses, I would be able to help more dogs through storytelling, and be able to build a real community for like-minded people and animal lovers – and I would need that amazing community right behind me to scale up my plans. I couldn't help 10,000 dogs a month single-handedly. I needed to bring a lot more backup to the plan.

Perhaps the hardest debate in my head was about working, after spending the past year recovering from addiction. Did I have the energy and passion to apply myself again? As a recovering addict, who'd only been at death's door in ICU a year gone past, was I actually well enough?

How hands-on would I be? Where would it be located? There were hundreds of questions I didn't really have the answers to at that stage. But there was a purpose and a determination to work them out.

Closing the laptop and making sure Snoop had his last pee for the night before bed, I felt properly excited for the first time in a year, head buzzing with logistics, funding, business models, research.

I drifted off to sleep thinking of all the dogs I'd met, and dreaming of structures I'd have to put in place to give them all their best chance. It would be one hell of a journey, and I was now itching to get going.

The next morning, after feeding Snoop and taking the old boy out to stretch his legs, I went to buy a big bag of kibble ready to meet more hungry doggy mouths, for the first twenty or so dogs that needed it. I grinned to myself, thinking that in business talk, back in the old days, I would have announced in a meeting we have 'twenty Daily Active Users' or 'twenty happy customers'.

Only 9,980 to go each month after that, I smiled wryly, wondering if I was being foolishly optimistic.

Happily I managed to track down Lucky early on – tail wagging, little bell ringing, proudly sporting her jaunty bright collar around her newly cleaned golden fur. A collar is the surest sign a dog is cared for, and she seemed to be wearing it with pride, as if to say, 'Someone loves me now, look at me all being looked after.'

My heart swelled seeing her clever little face waiting for me, and I was able to give her the medicines the vet had prescribed. 'We'll get you back on track, my lovely Lucky,' I promised her, giving her neck a good old ruffle.

And many other dogs were all there waiting for me too, as they'd come to expect my scooter in the mornings, knowing it would lead to a belly full of food. Because all the dogs here breed with each other, it's not like they're pedigrees, there's a beautiful mix of all sorts of mutts. Very generally speaking, they're smallish, wiry, with short hair and brown or dark-coloured fur. So you don't really identify them by saying 'there's the black labrador' or the German shepherd, or spaniel, or bulldog, like you might talk about dogs back at home.

Instead, I'd started coming up with my own slightly silly ways of identifying the different packs I was feeding, like the Originals, the first pack of four dogs I met who lived at the top of the hill in the jungle. There was Mum, Dad and their two adorable puppies. All beautiful brown and black creatures with a bit of Alsatian in the mix from the look of it. Because they were so remote they were always absolutely starving. They were noble creatures, and exceptionally wary of people, but I was slowly winning them over one day at a time.

Then there was the pair I dubbed the Quiet Couple, an impeccably well-mannered husband and wife (or so I liked to imagine) duo who lived on the jungle's edge. Inseparable from each other, they were heart-meltingly adorable, and would always want hugs and cuddles from me after their dinner.

The Big Eared Puppies were identical beauties with comically large lug holes, hence the nickname. I thought they were a trio originally, until my friend Lana said there were actually three more. Sure enough, later in the week all six of the lively litter started showing up, enjoying typical large-family squabbles every day about who got to go first for dinner. There was Billy, who got his own name because he was all on his own, apparently Billy-no-mates. He pretty much stayed in town, beside a car wash, presumably for the easy access to water and the off chance of human scraps to hoover up. An absolute gentleman, he sported an old leg injury from some sort of accident I presumed. I didn't really like to think about what had happened. But it made me feel warm inside, seeing his weight improving visibly by the day, seeing him hold his head a little higher.

Wonky – if you saw her ears you'd know why this part-German shepherd sweetheart got her moniker – was another favourite. She loved two things in life … human affection and food. Because she only got them once a day she could never decide which one she wanted first. She'd dart around undecided. Aged about six I guessed, Wonky used to have her own humans according to some locals, but had ended up being a street dog. Sadly, this is a common scenario. Dogs can be abandoned if the owners no longer have the finances to feed or care for them. I knew Wonky would absolutely thrive if I could find her another human family one day, she had so much love to give. I had to make re-homing part of the bigger plan too.

The Family of Five weren't on the dog run originally, but the two young blond pups chased me one day on the moped and begged for the last of my food, pushing their little black snouts into the near-empty sack of kibble. The next day they invited their whole family along – with their fairly dopey dad who'd clearly been in a few fights – and the whole brood soon became a firm fixture.

There were many others – the Mountain pack, the Dirt Track pack, the Big Trees pack, Mr and Mrs Fox (no prizes for guessing what they looked like). Plus one I nicknamed Old Boy, a timid older gent who was desperately grateful for a meal and had a slightly Eeyorish demeanour.

There was one I dubbed Happy, a handsome lad with white fur and black patches, a bit like a Friesian cow, and big brown eyes that looked like they'd been circled with black kohl eye pencil. Quite simply, this guy was always happy. He even tried to kind of speak to me and make real noises as if he was saying 'thanks Niall' when I rustled up his own coconut 'plate' for dinner. *You're welcome, Happy*, I grinned at him.

A dog I called Marlon Brando was also one of the canines I met and fed from very early on and took under my wing. I called him that because he was older, probably 12 I'd say, and he had a definite gravitas about him. He was greying a little, his eyesight had certainly faded and he was a little slower on his feet. Like the Hollywood legend he was named after, I liked to imagine he was the Godfather – or Dogfather – of canines. A Street Dog Named Desire, back in the day, just like the real Marlon Brando.

The fact that he'd clearly spent all his life as a street dog deserved my respect; it's a tough life and this boy had proved he was a gutsy survivor. He was a jolly and wise soul. Despite being past his peak, he seemed to have a certain gratitude for whatever he had left. The perfect example of a creature living in the moment. I've learned during my time with them that dogs really do this better than anyone. They don't beat themselves up with regrets like we do.

Marlon Brando was quite a big old boy. In his prime he would have been one of the stronger dogs and would have had decent muscle and power in his younger days. But like humans, his physical abilities had faded with the advancing years.

But he never let his mature age beat him. It was as if he was proud of the fact he'd come this far despite the odds stacked against him. 'Give some respect to your elders, kids,' he seemed to say with his canine swagger. 'There's life in this old dog yet.' Quite an admirable attitude to ageing, I felt!

Marlon Brando was clearly a little stiff in his bones, but he maintained a jaunty enough walk. He would hang at the back of his pack mainly but come trotting out to meet me when he heard the bike's distinctive *put-put-put* noise. He had an infectious joie de vivre about him and still plenty of beans left.

What you find with older dogs like Marlon Brando is, they get pushed down the pecking order of the pack. No other dogs were bullying him, he was never going to be anyone's victim, but he was no longer the top dog he once would have been in his youth. That's just the normal order of life. Stronger dogs take over. Just as in the human world the younger generation is handed the baton by their elders. Then the older ones are put out to pasture.

So Marlon Brando would patiently wait his turn when it came to the food I was handing out. And I was always keen for him to get fed, knowing he might not be pushing himself forward as greedily as the youngsters. I'd keep an eye on him and lead him to the meals once the others had pushed off to play. Dogs don't exactly have impeccable table manners; they don't hang around discussing their days politely while waiting for the last dog to finish eating, as we feel obliged to do after a meal.

He seemed in pretty good health for his years, all things considered. The only thing that was clearly deteriorating was his eyesight. I could tell he was going blind and while I was sure he could still see outlines and shapes, his vision was obviously compromised. He was street smart though, and used his sense of smell and wily ways to keep him out of trouble.

I'd noticed that his eyes would be filled with 'sleep' or gunk. That slightly sticky thing you sometimes get in the corners when you wake up. He seemed to have it constantly and of course wasn't able to wipe it away with his paws.

I'd started packing some simple supplies on my bike, including some baby wipes, and I used these to give his little eyes a gentle clean up before he had his meal. He seemed to really appreciate the hand I was lending him, and he'd even nudge at my leg with his snout, then look up at me squinting and blinking. The gesture made me smile. 'Yes Marlon Brando, I'm here to do your eyes old boy,' I'd reassure him.

I did this small, simple thing for him every single day. It wasn't a big deal. It wasn't a heroic act. It didn't involve vet bills or dramatic rescues. But it was very satisfying knowing that a tiny thing I could offer, just a few seconds of tenderly wiping his eyes for him, would make a real positive difference to the rest of his day.

It felt significant to me, because without fail I showed up and I was there for Marlon Brando. It made me think of all the times in my life when I hadn't actually behaved so responsibly or reliably. When I hadn't shown up for people, like I should have done, who deserved my attention.

In my drinking days I had always been incredibly unreliable, making excuses not to meet people so I could drink. I made excuses not to work so I could drink. I made excuses not to get out of bed, so I could drink. I frequently lied to people, went missing, I failed to show up, I was unpredictable, I let people down constantly – all so I could drink. How I acted was shameful.

So the fact that I turned up for Marlon Brando, every single day, made me feel a tiny bit proud of myself and the progress I'd made since sorting my shit out. It wasn't much, but it felt symbolic. I'd become reliable now. A human who could actually be trusted to do the right thing and could now commit to something selfless.

The leader of Marlon Brando's pack was another dog I fed called Bubba, who was aged around 8 I'd say. A huge, larger-than-life character and another natural-born survivor on the street, and a wily dog too. One time Bubba sliced his paw and needed the vet to put in six stitches. Dogs cut themselves all the time unfortunately, often it heals by itself, but when Bubba went limp and was totally out of sorts, it was clear he needed the vet.

Sure enough, it was diagnosed that Bubba had sepsis. This infection can be very deadly, but thankfully he'd been caught in time. Further blood tests showed that Bubba also had major kidney issues, blood parasites and abnormal blood levels.

These things could all be sorted out however, and I ended up taking Bubba back to my place while he recovered. He'd clearly never been in a house before in his life and was confused. He didn't pee the whole time, bless him, not sure where to go but sensing it wouldn't be welcome on my floor. And he seemed nervous about Snoop, not that he needed to be. He's a right softy. But he was conscious of being in someone else's territory.

Thankfully, I was able to sort Bubba out, and once he was back to full health he was happy to go back on to the streets and be leader of the pack once more. Dogs like Bubba can do just fine with no owners, they can get by on their wits, but even they need a little helping hand sometimes and I was happy to get him back on his paws.

Bubba is one of the smartest dogs I've ever met. There was one time when he started walking with a limp. Worried, we had it thoroughly investigated at the vet's … and discovered absolutely nothing wrong with his leg. He had only worked out that if he walked with a limp he'd get more attention and some extra treats. In fact, on watching him closely, we realised he would sometimes 'forget' about his limp once he'd had his treats! We fell about laughing.

You have to take your hat off to super-intelligent dogs like our Bubba, they need all their wits about them if they're to survive.

I was beginning to feel so fond of all of the dogs, they were such characters. It was Lucky who came first though, my favourite girl. She would race out to greet me excitedly on hearing the moped. The meds were going down a treat, her skin was looking vastly improved and my aim was to get her big and strong. All her ailments were totally treatable.

I still worried about her being such a loner, even though I frequently tried to introduce her to other dogs. There was safety in numbers, I felt, but she had no interest. She just wanted to be on her own all the time. She liked to keep on the patch she was on, which was a radius of about 400 metres. There were other dogs on the same patch she could easily have interacted with, and some would try to come to play with her and try and draw her in, but she always doggedly stuck by herself. Still, I would keep on trying …

I'd taken all these dogs into my heart, they relied on my visits now. And I couldn't let them down. These animals put a smile on my face and filled my damaged heart with pure joy.

It seemed that word was very much out on the doggy grapevine that there was a bald white-headed Irishman driving around in the midday sun with a bag of the good stuff, because more and more dogs began appearing over the weeks.

SEVEN

NOT EVERY BATTLE CAN BE WON

I met Tyson only about three weeks after I had started feeding the dogs and he remains a huge part of what I do and why I still do it today. I wish I knew more about him to tell you. All I can say is that he wasn't in my life for long, yet he made an important impact. My experience with Tyson perfectly sums up that wise old saying, 'It's the moments in life and not the minutes that count.'

He was the first dog I tried some medical care on myself, and I have used what I learned from him almost every day since then. He came into my life because I got two calls about him, one from a volunteer with Samui Street Dogs, who are a group of ex-pats like me dedicated to improving the lives of dogs, and one from my friend Lana, another hugely devoted dog person, who was out walking. They both told me they had seen a dog appear on the jungle road who was clearly very sick. It seemed that the dog had been dumped there as neither Lana nor the other volunteer had seen this dog before. You do get to recognise the faces after a while. And this boy seemed to have appeared from nowhere. I went up to see if I could find him and investigate.

It didn't take me long to track this newcomer down, and he was certainly in a bad way. We were all a bit scared of him to be honest; he had a massive swollen head and looked terrible, swaying unsteadily on his feet. I was still incredibly new to caring for dogs at this stage and was really just feeding them kibble. I didn't really know how to properly look after them apart from that, let alone how to treat them when they were sick.

It was immediately clear that he was very ill. Not just with cuts and minor injuries typical of strays. This was serious. He was quite small, sandy coloured and had a black muzzle and sharp ears that sat up proudly on his head, which was frighteningly swollen to almost twice the size that it should be. The severely expanded head was clearly impacting his breathing, so all I could do initially was sit with him and gently touch his head and ears. He seemed to be labouring to catch his breath, which was irregular. I was trying to think about what could have landed him in this sad state. Had he had a snake bite? Had he been hit by a vehicle? Did he have brain damage? I just couldn't figure it out, and was really struck that I simply didn't know enough about dogs to be able to piece it together. I've realised it's like being a detective half the time working with injured dogs, and I wasn't experienced at the job.

I knew he needed help quickly though with such dramatic swelling, so I put him into an old wooden crate and got him to the vet's. They agreed that he was extremely ill and hooked him up to some fluids and gave him some anti-inflammatory medicines to help the swelling and settle him down. He stayed overnight on a drip and then, not having anywhere else to take him, I brought him home with me. I hoped that the swelling would come down and he would start to feel better and be able to take some food and fluids himself and perhaps recover from there.

That first night back at mine he was still pretty bad. He could lap a little bit of water I brought up to his slackened mouth for him, but he was clearly exhausted and slept a lot. Even though I could not do much for him medically, it felt the right thing to have brought him in off the roads, which would have been frightening in his state. I might not know how he'd come to be there, but I felt pretty certain he'd been left to die there.

This is quite common when a dog is very sick in Thailand. I knew that if I hadn't brought him in he would have run out of water and food, had no medical care and would have died alone and in pain. A horrible way for anyone to leave this world. Even now, when I have been doing what I do for over a year, I don't know how people can live with that behaviour on their consciences. Like if animals were out of sight they'd be out of mind? It was unfair and I didn't want this for him. Or any other dog for that matter.

When he had been at home with me and Snoop for a day or so, wrapped up in warm blankets, I had begun to see some slow improvement. He was drinking water and eating himself. Then things really changed. He properly perked up, took some steps, began to wag his tail and I could see some life back in his keen black eyes. 'Hey, you're feeling better!' I cried, giving him a gentle kiss on the slightly less poorly looking head.

I really hoped he was making a comeback, and I felt positive. I even decided to name him Tyson after the boxer Tyson Fury. Fury's long career has been a rollercoaster. He's had mental and physical health problems and run-ins with the press. He's been truly down and out, spread-eagled on the canvas both literally and metaphorically, and yet he has come back and rebuilt his life and career. Tyson, I decided, was a fitting name for this dog who had apparently fought his way back to health so heroically. I was determined to allow him to have a great and glorious comeback like his namesake.

I felt so excited I posted the good news online. I really do try and keep the mood upbeat and light on my social feeds and in my newsletters. There's enough misery in the world out there already. Why add to the gloom? I want to make people feel good and give them a lovely hit of dopamine when they're scrolling through their feeds while sitting on the tube or bus, or waiting to pick the kids up, or having a coffee break. I wanted everyone to share in the joy of Tyson's remarkable turnaround.

It looked absolutely like that was happening. Tyson had started to eat, lapping away at some homemade broth and even taking some solids. His head swelling had started to go down and he was chewing nicely. I was still worried because there was no clear diagnosis after the vet had inspected him, so I felt we didn't really know what we were dealing with, but he was comfortably wrapped up in blankets and duvets on my floor, and seemingly doing well. I lay down close to him, listening and watching his movements, my confidence growing that he was going to recover. *This is fantastic. The medicine is kicking in and I'm going to save this dog* … I was on a real high. It was almost like it was easy. Maybe I had the knack after all?

Looking back on it, I was stupidly hopeful. I was living inside that hope, willing Tyson to recover. Yet on his third night with me at my apartment, hope went out the window … and the harsh reality of life replaced it.

I woke up at four o'clock in the morning, and I was lying on the floor with Tyson beside me. His breathing was really short and laboured, air catching in his throat, not quite filling his lungs like it should. Worst of all, he was agitated. He scrambled himself up to standing and was pacing back and forth. This was so different to earlier in the day, something was now seriously wrong.

There are no Thai vets available out of hours really. So in the middle of the night I gave him – and myself – a little pep talk.

Right. We're going to have to get through this together, Tyson, and we'll get you back to the vet's first thing in the morning, old boy. We'll get to the bottom of this, hang on in there buddy.

But by five in the morning things were only worse. Tyson's breathing had become shallower and he lay listlessly on the cold floor tiles of my apartment. He'd shrugged off the covers and shuffled himself to the corner of the room, as if to slip away quietly. As I tried to get water into him, I was looking at the wall clock slightly desperately.

Jesus, I've got to get him to 9 am so we can get to the vet's.

But by the time the clock turned seven I had a moment of clarity. I think now it was one of the most important realisations I've had since I started this work: there was no comeback now. I knew Tyson was going to die.

I didn't know much about dogs then. I didn't know about medicine or veterinary care, but I knew instinctively what suffering looked like, and this was suffering of a different type. My gut feeling told me that these were the last hours of Tyson's life, and he was going to die here in my little apartment before I could take him anywhere to get help.

At that time I think I probably saw it as giving in, and failing him, but I've come to realise since then that I learned an important life lesson that dawn morning: my love and heartfelt care were the only things he needed at that moment. Rather than trying to change what was clearly playing out in front of me, I had to accept it. That was more important now. To give him my love and allow him to pass in peace.

I made Tyson as comfortable as I could, I rearranged my best blankets around his shivering body, moved him into a light and peaceful room and got the air-conditioning on him. I sat there for the next hour or so and just held his sandy-coloured paw and talked to him. I told him about my plans for the dogs of Thailand, and stories about my life. I did all of this knowing, deep in my bones, that he was just about to die.

I had seen dead people, and I had seen dogs who had died, but I had never really been with someone who was in the process of death itself, experiencing up close as life ebbed away from the street dog.

The final minutes of Tyson's life were hard to watch. His little body started to shake, his legs went up in the air and he went stiff. I held his paw tighter and felt, very deeply, that this was one of the first times I was really proud of myself since I had given up alcohol and fought through my depression. I had never had this level of responsibility for somebody else, or stood up to care for someone in this way.

My former life was always about being selfish, about lying to get my next drink, about making excuses for my actions, excuses for my failings. But now I was there for this soul as he passed. It felt like Tyson was absolutely reinforcing everything that I wanted to do, and I told him very clearly that I was going to do hard and incredible work in his name. Finally, I said to him, 'People will remember you, Tyson.'

I kept my hand on him to show he was not alone until his body had long stopped rising and falling with any breaths. After Tyson passed, I sat there for about half an hour. The experience left me completely drained.

Tyson had really got under my skin, I know it sounds silly, he was only a dog I'd known for such a short amount of time. But I was genuinely as emotional as if a human had died in front of me.

Also, there was a practical issue I had no idea about. I didn't have a clue what I was going to do with the body. Was I supposed to cremate him? Take him up to the mountains to bury him? I asked my Thai neighbours for advice and they were so lovely. 'We will bury him in the garden,' they told me, which is the normal custom for beloved animals. 'We will help you.'

So later that day, one of my Thai neighbours and I dug Tyson a grave together in my little back garden. We buried him there beneath a simple formation of four rocks and I laid strong-stemmed flowers with bright orange blooms against the stones. I still regularly go out into the garden and tell Tyson how things are going. I tell him if it has been a long hard day. I tell him if I have had setbacks. I tell him about the small wins that have helped other dogs or my friends. I tell Tyson everything because he's a big part of why I do this.

I guess lots of people might think it's strange that a dog with whom I spent only about 72 hours could have such a monumental impact on me. He died next to me, and I felt like I made his death as comfortable and dignified as it possibly could have been. Many other people would have driven past him, or left him at the vet's among other sick animals he didn't know, but I held his paw until the end and gave him what I could.

I can't pretend these things don't affect me. One of the best things about being sober is having a clear head to think things through. And the energy to actually get up and do them. But I can still suffer from depression and anxiety. I can still doubt myself and feel scared about the journey of saving 10,000 dogs each month that I'd pledged to undertake.

My fears wouldn't come across on social media where I try to keep it all positive for people. But fundamentally here I was, living in a country which I know nothing about, trying to build something important when I can't even speak Thai. But I was determined to start this new endeavour from scratch, and without a network here to lean on. I knew it was going to be the biggest challenge of my life. I was having to get educated on medical treatments, and in all honesty I could feel a little squeamish with some of the injured dogs. I felt like I didn't have a clue.

Every time I got struck with fear and self-doubt I'd take myself off for a jungle walk or curl up with Snoop on the sofa and calm myself down. I tried to stay positive and visualise how it might all work one day in five years' time. I would stand on top of the mountain overlooking the jungle and visualise in detail the facility I wanted to eventually build, with hundreds of dogs, vets coming and going, trucks loading up with food, smiling faces and dogs wagging their tails. I found this technique helped me. You should give it a go if you get anxiety too.

Another trick I always tried to take away from the rising fear was to think about the worst-case scenario. What would that look like and involve? Would people laugh at me for failing? I had to decide, so what if they did? I couldn't let that stop me from having a go. My personal worst-case scenario, I decided, was that this whole project doesn't work, it falls flat on its arse and I look stupid for publicly saying I could save 10,000 dogs a month. I realised if that was the case, I would just go back to feeding and helping ten dogs a day and driving around with the Koh Samui sunshine beating on my back. I realised, in the grand scheme of things, that wouldn't be so bad. I just needed to pick myself up and carry on.

★ ★ ★

Tyson's death was a harsh setback, but it made me realise that I had so much to give and so much more to grow. And it was mainly going well. Lucky continued to make excellent progress and was coming every day for her food and her meds, which were almost finished. In the past, whenever I'd had to get pills down Snoop, I'd make an effort to grind them down or hide them in his food. But I knew that this kind of approach wasn't practical on a wider scale, and with some street dogs sharing food it would be impossible to make sure the right ones were getting the medicines they needed.

So I mastered the art of opening Lucky's mouth, sliding in the pills and getting her to comfortably swallow them before her breakfast. The trust between us was well established. As her health improved she became like a new dog, no longer whippet thin, just lean and full of life and vitality. I took her to the beach one day and she ran up and down the sand excitedly which filled me with ridiculous amounts of joy as well as hope for the future about what could be achieved.

I filmed her grinning (I know, strictly speaking dogs can't grin, but I like to think she can) and running the length of the beach (behind the camera I was certainly grinning and running beside her trying to keep up) and then posted the video online. People could not believe it was the same dog. I was over the moon with her progress.

I'd also had a surprising breakthrough with finding her

a pal. Chopper, named after his helicopter-like tail, was an adorable little pup who was found in one of the abandoned houses, one of the little shacks where coconut farmers would come and live whenever the fruit was ripe.

One of the construction workers must have brought the puppy with them and just left him there maybe. Or someone else seemed to think Chopper did actually have a family looking out for him, but they were rarely around. Who knows? But the little thing had such an infectious personality, tail always wagging madly, a real livewire. He eventually wore even Lucky the loner down, she simply couldn't be aloof and standoffish when Chopper was begging her to play with him. After four or five days of him refusing to take no for an answer, they were inseparable. I was overjoyed to see them pair up and Lucky find a companion at last.

These two were extremely happy, well fed, sheltered and loved their jungle spot. As street dogs go, they had a set-up fit for royalty.

EIGHT

WHY PUPPIES ARE BAD

After a few weeks I was up to feeding forty-odd dogs per day, which I felt was the limit of what I could manage single-handedly. It was still as fulfilling and enjoyable as ever driving through the jungle, feeling the warm rays on my face, being greeted by wagging tails. I had real bonds with so many of them.

But 'my dogs' were all within about a one-mile radius. There were thousands more on Koh Samui alone, and millions of stray dogs across all of Thailand. If I thought about trying to make a meaningful difference, it was hard not to feel overwhelmed. Especially with the discovery of more and more dogs.

During the late spring and early summer 'puppy season' kicked into action. This is when they all tend to come at once, and not only that ... people had started dumping unwanted pups in exactly the places where they knew I would find them. It's usually the female puppies that are dumped, as most people only want to keep the males who won't reproduce themselves, so avoiding further hassle and more mouths to feed.

I found eleven puppies, from two different litters, within the same 100-metre stretch of road. You'd need a heart of stone to abandon them, so they also became added to my dog-feeding route. Female dogs can be mature enough to produce litters when they're just seven to eight months old and still babies themselves really. So you can see why the problems just get out of hand when the dogs are multiplying at such a rapid rate.

The sheer size of the problem and the relentlessness of new dogs appearing could easily get you down. Because just by keeping these puppies alive, it means stopping everything else you're planning in terms of helping to fix the bigger picture.

After a bit of research, I learned that goat's milk was a nutritious drink for the youngsters, either a replacement for their mummies' milk or just as a supplement. The sight of excited puppies lapping up milk, contented tiny tails all wagging, is honestly one of the most joyous things I've witnessed in life.

And I try to savour those special moments because otherwise I would just bemoan the puppy situation endlessly. They are expensive to look after compared to the older dogs (I reckon each one I find is about $200 to save if you include sterilising, medicine, goat's milk, food, transport, care and other things). It doesn't sound like a lot but when you multiply it, soon adds up.

I started buying the milk by the gallon, in case the mums

needed some help with feeding them, or worse – the mothers had left the pups to fend for themselves.

I had a close call with Angel, a street dog I found living beside a busy road who had eight puppies. Bless her, she was constantly trying to protect them from the traffic, but it was only a matter of time before they would get hit. While the three cutest puppies were adopted by locals, Angel was still left with the other five puppies, who were – sadly – deemed less desirable. Although they were given food and goat's milk twice a day their chances on the busy road were never good, though Angel did her best and at least they had a loving mummy.

But when Angel vanished one day, leaving the poor puppies to fend for themselves, their chances of survival dramatically decreased. For four days I was terrified for their future. With other volunteers I hatched a plan to try and move the puppies somewhere safe … and then a miracle happened as Angel was finally found – thanks to a Facebook post – on the other side of the island.

We'll never know how she got there, but it almost brought tears to my eyes when we were able to move mum and pups together to a safe place beside the sea, away from traffic, where they could be cared for daily. Two kind-hearted locals even created little houses for them. Their own seaside villas! Food, water and shelter. I was made up seeing them all safe and knowing their future was far brighter all together with their mummy.

But that was just one story with a happy ending. How could I carry on at this pace? It's one thing when the dogs are puppies, because everyone loves a puppy, they're cute and fluffy and adorable. Humans are more likely to throw them scraps when they're little. But the reality is that puppies will mostly all have a hard life ahead. Many will die young, their lives can be brutally fleeting, and in the meantime they'll have a miserable time searching for food and quite likely battling illness.

As they naturally don't understand the road dangers yet, there's a high chance that some of the puppies will be hit by a passing car or motorbike. Their protective mums might have the instinct to shield them as best they can by barking at cars, but if there are seven puppies in the litter, well, even the best mummy in the world can't keep them all safely away from the traffic.

It's not just cars these youngsters have to avoid, here there are also cobras, parasites and humans who want rid of them. If a developer or resort owner is building a new block of flats or a hotel, they don't want smelly looking street dogs lurking around lowering the tone. Many dogs and pups end up victims of poisons laid down specifically for them to eat.

It seems especially cruel to know that many of these puppies would sell for $1,000 each in other countries, where they'd likely be cherished pets leading healthy and safe lives. Here in Thailand, they have to somehow just manage to survive against all the odds. It is not a fair life at all.

Then the females quickly start attracting male attention when they go into season themselves, and so the cycle continues. It's brutal. Just when you think you are getting on top of feeding and nursing, along comes another batch. They seem to come from everywhere – you find them by the road, in the jungle, down holes and in abandoned shacks.

Dealing with puppy season needs all hands on deck, and I'm so grateful to all the people who help me with this. There are people who help me look after the puppies overnight. People who build little shelters. People who drive puppies around. Others who help me look for homes (this is always the ideal and the longest shot, but we give it a try). Then there are people who feed and give the puppies medicine as they grow.

In short, every time I discover even two more puppies I have to scour my WhatsApp groups and rustle up a small army of people just for those two tiny puppies that require a lot of attention.

Although it sounds counterintuitive for someone like me who loves dogs, it was clear my wider mission to help them had to absolutely prioritise stopping as many puppies being born as possible. Feeding the dogs was a good start but was barely the tip of the iceberg. The dog population needed to be controlled to stop the cycle of suffering. Feeding the dogs itself, I decided, was about as effective as trying to treat a heart attack with a sticking plaster.

In fact, I found myself wondering at times whether feeding them – while undoubtedly well meaning – was very naive and making the whole situation worse. After all, by feeding the dogs you're making them stronger, and therefore healthier and more likely to breed.

It's a tricky one, and there are many different arguments, all with some valid points. There is no manual out there instructing people on how best to manage the street-dog situation in Thailand. It's been like this for decades before I came along. I felt the only thing I could really do was follow my instinct. I just couldn't walk away from these animals in dire need of a meal, but at the same time I had to lay plans to stop this cycle by neutering and spaying the dogs which would improve their quality of life.

But just how logistically challenging would this be to execute? I tried to think it all through. It would cost about $40 to $50 to sterilise, but then there is the aftercare, for they need several days of medicine post-treatment to make sure they don't get infections, and then the stitches from the operation needed taking out. Would this even be possible trying to do en masse? How would I even catch them? I needed to find out for myself what could and couldn't be achieved.

To work out what would be possible, as a kind of trial run I set about capturing one of the smaller, friendlier dogs from the jungle, who I called Mr Fox.

There were three of them in his pack, Mr Fox, Mrs Fox and Aunty Fox, because they were all a reddy-brown, all had pointy little snouts and pricked-up ears and a wolfy sort of grin, too. Mr Fox was the gentlest of souls, I could tell that by how he was with the others, never an ounce of aggression, so a good one to practise on.

I was nervous about how it would work out. But after luring him in with the promise of food, little Mr Fox came willingly towards me, like he knew I had his best interests at heart. 'Alright, Niall,' he seemed to be shrugging. 'I'm trusting you mate on this one.' I was careful not to make any sudden movements, and he was easy enough and small enough to grab. He didn't want to be coaxed into the basic box I'd borrowed from a friend, but he happily sat next to me, while I patted him and kept him calm as we drove the thirty-minute journey to the vet's. I also relied on a friend's car loan.

I'm really going to have to buy my own jeep if I'm going to be doing more of this ...

The vet sorted out poor Mr Fox's testicles quickly enough, it was all super straightforward, and during the simple operation the vet marked the dog's ear with a little 'V' tattoo. This would mean that if anyone found Mr Fox at any later stage, perhaps another volunteer, they'd know he'd already been neutered. It would be a crying waste if he was put under anaesthetic only for them to discover he's already been taken care of in that department. Vets can use different little signs, not always a 'V', but any small tattoo in the ear generally means the same thing.

After his recovery from the operation, Mr Fox went safely back into the jungle a few hours later, with his meds inside him to ward off any potential infection post op, and I promised to take him back to the vet to have a check-up and have his stitches removed in a few days' time.

The whole procedure, happily, had been a success – and most important of all, it meant Mr Fox would not be able to father any more puppies with Mrs Fox, Aunty Fox, or any other lovely lady dogs on the island for that matter. We had stopped potentially hundreds more puppies from having to survive out there.

I gave him lots of food and strokes to make up for being made infertile. 'Sorry fella,' I smiled at him, 'but I promise you it's really for the best.'

It was good to know that capturing the street dogs was possible. The only way to manage doing this work is by staying positive and upbeat. Fix the problem in front of you and quickly move on to the next part of the puzzle. All I had to do now was several thousand more of them … but it was a start and an important step in the right direction.

★   ★   ★

By this time I was spending about $2,000 a month of my own money on the dog mission, on food, vet bills and medicines. I could manage that, and I was keen to always keep spending that amount personally, as well as giving all my time. This is exactly what I wanted to be doing.

But I knew that if I wanted to achieve my ambitious plan to neuter and really make a long-term, wider-picture difference, I needed more resources. I was constantly being offered cash from people who had seen my posts on social media and really wanted to get involved. I couldn't believe how supportive everyone was. I guess people really just love dogs even if they are halfway across the world. The community was there behind me, and with their generosity and kindness and shared love of dogs, I knew we could help so many more.

Right from the first time I posted about the dogs I had at least fifty people messaging me asking to donate to help. I was so touched, but before I could accept donations I needed to get everything in place logistically, and was all legally sound, to make sure I was doing everything correctly.

By the start of April 2022 I had everything in place to begin accepting donations from the community, with an online donorbox, and I also felt it was important for people to see how and what the money would be spent on, namely neutering fifty dogs a month, feeding many more a day, buying preventative medicines and taking more dogs like Lucky to the vet.

I explained that $5 could feed ten of the dogs and $500 would neuter ten, which would save hundreds more doggy lives in the long run. I asked for $4,000, but the donations just rolled in – within a week I'd received $8,000 and every single cent, dollar, pound and euro was put to good use sterilising dogs.

It felt so humbling to be trusted to do this with other people's money. It gave me drive and made me vow to honour my commitments as they were backing me so generously. I couldn't let anyone down.

I bought a banged-up old jeep, as I couldn't keep borrowing cars to take dogs to the vet, and I sourced two animal carriers so I could immediately crack on with the neutering programme. There was no time to waste if I needed to reach the fifty dogs a month target I'd set. I was full of wonderful nervous energy; it felt like my first day at school or the very first time I walked into a kitchen when I was training to be a chef. It was exciting, knowing that I was now fifteen months sober, had rebuilt my life, and here I was now putting an important plan into action.

It was only fitting that the very first dog I took was Angel. I was determined she wouldn't be going through another ordeal like she had with her puppies. Even just eight weeks after giving birth she was getting male interest and we couldn't afford to let her have any more. The operation went smoothly, and a vet friend taught me how to remove the post-op stitches myself, using a nail clipper. It was a useful tip as it meant fewer trips back to the vet, freeing up time to help more dogs. There were always plenty who needed it.

At the time of writing this book, so far I've sterilised 350 dogs since the start of April 2022, and thanks to great partners and donations I am now doing fifty dogs a month. But it's exhausting and relentless.

When you get a day in puppy season when you're finding fifty puppies, I'll be honest, I can feel like weeping in frustration. But then someone's kindness restores your faith in humanity. Like my new local young friend, Chris, who uses a wheelchair. He could see I was having a hard time catching dogs to sterilise; it's never easy as the street dogs don't trust where you're going to take them.

After a lot of failed attempts – and two hours without being able to get a single dog – this little boy waved me over. He said he had dogs and led us around the migrant workers' camp, speeding his wheelchair around to different groups of dogs who were all friendly with him. He helped us easily catch seven dogs in just twenty minutes. All done with a smile on his face and huge excitement at being involved. He didn't want anything in return for his time, he was just delighted to have helped, but I made sure he had a few token notes pressed into his palm so he could go to the sweet shop. When I went back to my vehicle later, someone had sweetly put some onions there for me. It's people like him who absolutely keep my spirits buoyed up when I need it.

Kids in general are great for reassuring the dogs and helping us catch them. The dogs trust those kids. They are their friends. It got me thinking about how the innocence of children and puppies often gets lost with the harsh reality of life. Young kids and puppies can be so pure. It's us older humans that often mess them up somehow.

I know that logistically it would be better to just focus on sterilising alone, instead of doing all the other things I do like organising food for 800 dogs, looking after sick dogs and rescuing pups. But then your phone lights up with a new message: 'I see you have been flat out and are tired, Niall, but we have a problem ...'

Although I am grateful there are people caring about the dogs, it's hard not to feel your heart sink on receiving those messages ... *More puppies, really?* But you would need a heart of stone to hear that noise of a puppy scared and whimpering and looking for its mum and then not feel like you had to do something.

It's very hard to stop the flow of new dogs, and it's a big, complicated problem to solve on many levels. But I can't walk away, all I can do is keep them safe and fed, give them vaccinations – and sterilisations when they are old enough – to give them a much better chance at life. It feels an impossible task to look for homes but that's what is needed.

One thing I HAVE learned is not to try and catch dogs for sterilising in the bad weather. The dogs all hide when it's wet for one thing, and for another it slows down the whole process as there's more traffic and we need to keep drying the volunteers out, etc. I've learned to start checking the forecast these days.

People often ask me whether I've been bitten by a dog. Until just recently, a year after I started out, I would always slightly smugly reply 'no'. But perhaps inevitably, it was always going to happen. It was while I was trying to catch dogs to sterilise, and I guess I got too complacent.

There was a big, nervous white boy, he looked a little bit retriever-like, with some German shepherd in there, and I *thought* he was safely sedated. We buy the sedation pills from the vet. Sedating them is often necessary but can be risky as you're never sure if they've had enough. So I thought he was sleeping and snuck up behind him to grab him and transport him to the vet. Clearly this wasn't wise! He very much wasn't fully asleep and understandably I panicked him with my sudden movement.

It was a silly error on my part. The dog quickly got a good grip on my right arm and I went down as if I'd been shot, screaming like a baby.

I knew with bites that early treatment was crucial, and someone drove me straight to the same private hospital where I had been in ICU two years before. I had it all cleaned up, a few stitches and a couple of jabs for rabies (even though it's not on the island, it seemed sensible) and tetanus and antibiotics.

I didn't let it get me down, and certainly didn't let it put me off. People were so kind and quick to offer to help, even people who had never fed a dog before said they'd step in to do my feeding round.

That bite might have been inconvenient, but at the end of the day six more dogs had been sterilised and vaccinated and moved from the dangerous dual carriageway where they were living. It really wasn't the dog's fault, he was scared and just reacting instinctively. I even took the fella a few sausages the next day to show there were no hard feelings.

NINE

WHO DO YOU TAKE HOME WHEN YOU CAN'T TAKE THEM ALL?

Jumbo was an elderly street dog living on his own on a busy road under a food cart. He was covered in ticks and fleas, as they mostly all are. The horrible ticks get in the ears and between the paws and anywhere on the body where it's warm. It's revolting and horribly uncomfortable for the dogs. But with basic medicine that you feed to the dogs, you can get rid of the ticks within 24 hours normally.

Jumbo also had badly swollen legs, the size of inflated party balloons. But after only a couple of trips to the vet to get some anti-inflammatory medicine, a good powdering session to de-flea him, a bath to clean him, plus plenty of nutritious food, the turnaround in just seven days was incredible.

He had kidney issues that needed treating, but his legs started getting back to normal and I decided to treat him to a beach day with Snoop. I hoped that the salt water would ease his legs a bit, but he was happy to watch Snoop splash and sit on the sand instead. The pair of them got on so well that they were soon inseparable and would curl up to sleep together.

Knowing Jumbo was old, over ten, and seeing how much his quality of life had improved in just the week he'd stayed with me, I knew I wouldn't have the heart to see him back on the streets.

I'd also learned from asking around locally that Jumbo had originally had a home with foreigners, but they'd left him behind when they fled the country when Covid struck. (I know, how could they? But who knows what else they had going on in their lives.) Poor Jumbo had been a stray for two years. It seemed especially cruel knowing he had once had a good life and then had had to adjust to living on the streets.

Jumbo was so grateful to be comfortable that I decided he could see out the rest of his days at leisure with me and Snoop. I'd met him in the autumn of his life and I wanted to make some happy moments for him after he'd struggled for so long. Snoop and I both gladly welcomed the old boy into the gang.

But that was just one dog. There were so many more in need. Like Donatella, a gorgeous and gentle white street dog who was in a bad way and on the other side of the island living in a petrol station. She had badly infected private parts, the poor girl must have been in pain, lots of open wounds and was so weak she was struggling to stand. I was able to get her fixed up slightly myself, take her to the vet's, feed her and get her on the road to recovery with injections and medicines. But she was still 15 kilometres away and living on the streets. Someone in England offered to take her in, but I still had nowhere for her to go while she recovered. It really wasn't ideal for Donatella.

You might think, why don't you take Donatella home, Niall? Trust me, this is something I don't take lightly. It's the question that goes round and round in my head constantly. 'Who Do You Take Home?' That is such a tough choice when there are so many needy animals. It's the one that keeps me up at night and causes me severe anxiety. Your answer, if you were here too, with me and all the dogs, might be different to mine. The truth is there is probably no right answer.

As much as I would have liked to, I felt that taking dogs home would slow me down. My logic was that my time was better spent out in the 'field' finding more solutions en masse. I could easily take twenty dogs home but that doesn't solve anything. You could make a case for puppies in need, but then how could you leave injured dogs out there to fend for themselves? For the dogs who have been attacked, you worry, are you sending them to their death if you put them out on the streets after feeding them and addressing their basic medical requirements?

The daily picture is always changing on the island. New dog issues come into the frame on an hourly basis. A call from a tourist here, who has seen an injured dog; a message from a worried volunteer there who has seen a poorly dog that needs urgent treatment, or it will die. I want to help as many of them as I can, and sometimes this means simply getting them in the best shape healthwise as possible, before letting them back on the streets again.

People who live in America, England or Ireland frequently offer to take a dog and give it a home, which is wonderful and I'm so grateful for that. It does happen, but there is a long process involved and it's just not practical to ship out every dog from the environment they were born into. Having a 'failed' adoption, especially abroad, might be more harmful than keeping them on the streets in the environment they were born into.

The solution I will always return to, is to sterilise as many as I possibly can, and to put the fires out wherever they arise. It's not perfect and it is often life or death for a dog. But fundamentally, these are my reasons when some-one asks me … why don't you take the dog home with you?

I might not always get it right, and trust me, there are dark days when the depression hits and I question my every decision, but mainly I am going to bed at night and I know I have tried the very best I can.

What all this angst did make me realise though was that finding somewhere to home more dogs, like Jumbo and Donatella, must become my next priority. I wanted every dog to find their forever home, ideally with a loving family. But I knew that would take a long time and might not even be possible.

So I needed to create a safe place where they could stay while recuperating from illness, or spaying, or for some dogs a retirement home where they could see out the end of their days without having to scavenge for food and be infested with parasites.

I knew I needed to rent or buy the land and then construct some buildings to house dogs. Juggling everything from my jeep, moped and my small apartment just wasn't sustainable any more. I was spending way too much time driving sick animals around and having to put them back into very tricky situations on the streets. I was also spending a small fortune on keeping dogs in the vet's and various other places that needed paying. The only logical thing to do was to find some land and build a safe spot for the sickest and most needy dogs to recover. I needed a physical space. I just needed to find the right place.

I'd been visualising a place in my head for a few weeks, like a little doggie nirvana. Visualising things is what I do to keep myself motivated. But now I really needed to get my arse in gear and actually make it happen. To bring some clarity, I listed all the useful things we could do in a place like this. I always find it helps me to write plans down and share them with people in my newsletter or on my social media, it makes me feel more accountable. Once they are written and everybody knows about it, then I have to go and actually do it no matter how hard it might seem.

So I typed into my laptop one evening exactly why I needed a proper place. A special plot of land where:

- Dogs can recover and recuperate after procedures and/or illness.
- We can cook healthier food for the dogs en masse.
- Show the dogs to visitors (for potential new homes).
- Sterilise the dogs.
- Get dogs adopted.
- Educate people about dogs.

I imagined little trucks pulling in to collect food we had made on the premises. Volunteers walking dogs around the jungle. Happy people taking photos. A family picking a puppy. School classes visiting and learning about animals. And most of all, I visualised little dogs like Donatella, and so many others in need, being able to recover in a much safer place.

After drawing up my list and thinking about what was needed, I did the only sensible thing and arranged to meet people that week to start seeing some plots of land.

By May 2022, the dogs had taken over my life completely. Considering I'd only met Lucky and started feeding the first twenty dogs in January, in just a few short months, it had seemingly dominated my life and all my thoughts. But I've always been determined and focused when I needed to be, and once I'd got the bit between my teeth, I found it hard to stop. This new-found obsession with making a difference reminded me of being a single-minded kid in Belgium, practising my football drills again and again and again until I got better. Only this time, at 42, I had lived a lot of life and learned some important lessons along the way.

Starting this project was relatively easy for the first three months. It quickly grew to feeding eighty dogs a day, sterilising two dozen, re-homing three and fixing up a bunch of others who were very ill.

I couldn't help but fall back on my business way of thinking and looking at it in that way. I'd had what you'd call 'some smooth initial growth'. (That's a good thing by the way, though it sounds quite comical when talking about dogs I know.) But by May, in business terms, I had just hit the spot they call the 'messy middle'. It's the part of any project that feels tough when you're in it, you can't see your way out of it, but you feel it might be there if you can find your way through.

To put it simply, without the business jargon, my days were chock-a-block. And I knew that needed to change before I burned out and never achieved the bigger picture I felt would be possible one day.

Here is what my typical day (though there is no such thing really in this field of work) looked like, give or take a few dozen puppies or emergencies:

- 6.00 am. Wake up to feed and walk Snoop and Jumbo.
- 6.30 am. Shopping for supplies.
- 7.00–8.00 am. Feed eighty dogs.
- 8.00–9.30 am. Find and capture two dogs for sterilising + drive to vet.
- 9.30–10.30 am. Breakfast and answer messages (there were a LOT, and I really tried in these early months to reply to as many as possible).
- 10.30–12.00 am. Follow up with sick dogs, vet trips and medicines.
- 12.00–1.00 pm. Lunch and first social media posts. (These take time to edit and post, but people back in America, England or Ireland genuinely want to know how the dogs are doing, and it helps me feel connected to the dog-loving community. I'm on Instagram, Twitter and I make YouTube videos to educate all the kids about my work as some of them aren't allowed to use social media yet. The next step is to make them in Thai for the locals, but one step at a time …)
- 1.00–2.30 pm. In theory, this is my free time. (I try to sit in a cafe and treat myself to a pastry and coffee, my guilty pleasures. OK, I know eating pastry is not being healthy, but since I've given up booze, drugs, gambling and cigarettes I figure I deserve a little indulgence to spur me on.)
- 2.30–4.00 pm. Collect dogs from sterilising and return them.

- 4.00–5.00 pm. Walk and play with Snoop and Jumbo.
- 5.00–6.00 pm. Small second feeding round for sick dogs or puppies.
- 6.00–7.00 pm. Dinner and second social media posts. (I struggle with replying to messages on social media these days, but I hope the newsletters I send out give an overview of what I am doing and how I plan to help more dogs as quickly as possible. I LOVE hearing from the readers, it keeps me going, so please don't stop!)
- 7.00 pm onwards. In theory this is when I try to work on the bigger picture.

This 'typical day' will vary depending on whether it's the dreaded puppy season or some other curveball crisis comes up. I don't sterilise dogs every single day, but I am always looking for new ones, and it's logistically challenging as you've seen.

Making life or death decisions can take a massive toll on me and the other volunteers, and on our mental health. I really try to take care of that with some exercise, or a massage if I have a spare half hour, so as not to burn out. I certainly have a load more energy since quitting booze, thank God.

You don't need to be a genius to see why my love life has stalled … there's not much time for dating. I think at the back of my mind I know that my relationships have failed because of my drinking and commitment issues. And I know people who are avoiding getting hurt always trot out the hackneyed excuse about 'being too busy with work'.

But that really is the case here. It just feels like a particularly frantic time in my life. And I'm so happy to be doing this. I am absolutely open to meeting someone someday. But it's just not on the table. For now at least. You'd have to be a lunatic to want to be with me and all my anxieties and constant worries about the dogs. A girlfriend wouldn't see me for 23 hours of the day and a man carrying dog food around, driving a moped, smelling of dogs and not dressed very well isn't exactly a catch.

So holding down a relationship is far out of the realm of possibility at the moment and that's just the way it is. I've rebuilt myself from the ground up, and I am just too focused on our work.

I have to accept that the only special ladies in my life right now are the four-legged kind. Who knows, perhaps one day I'll find someone who wants to take this on, but finding her is not my priority. The dogs are.

Please don't think I'm moaning. It's a privilege to be here, surrounded by dogs in this tropical paradise. I am happier and more fulfilled than I have ever been. But I am still tired by the evenings. I get annoyed with myself that I haven't done some things a little faster but I keep getting stretched with dog emergencies. It's easy to say I'll focus on the great plans for the bigger picture, but then you bump into four puppies without a mother and you get pulled in another direction.

I have great intentions for 7 pm, and putting the bigger future plans into reality, but I am often so tired from the hectic and physical day that I often stare at my computer screen and am ready for bed at 8.30 pm.

Every time I sit down to have my dinner and read the messages I am blown away by the support. It would probably be quite a lonely endeavour were it not for social media and people urging me on. As well as the dogs, I feel like I don't want to let down all the people who support me. That feeds into being sober too. If I was to start drinking again, who would look after all the dogs and shoot videos to make people smile? The world would go on of course, but I like to use that thought to push me on every day. And if I can inspire anyone else to be kind towards dogs too, wherever they live in the world, then I'm a happy man.

TEN

THERE IS NO GREATER LOVE THAN A MOTHER'S

Beyoncé lived in the Koh Samui jungle, and she stumbled into my path one morning in April 2022, along with two other females, all hungry, beautiful and fierce. I don't mean fierce as in aggressive, they were anything but that, I just mean they were cool and sassy girls who often seemed to appear as an all-female trio. I nicknamed them Destiny's Child for that reason, though it was always Beyoncé who was the real standout star of the show for me.

Beyoncé had the most perfectly smooth fur, but boy, was she desperately thin. You don't get fat street dogs I know, but Beyoncé was pure skin and bones. You could count every rib on her and even her long face seemed drawn. She clearly wasn't an old dog, but she didn't have much strength.

She was hugely smart though, and as soon as she'd clocked my routine, she would trot out at seven each morning, head held high, bright eyes alert, eagerly sniffing for a meal. What's more, when food was put down in front of her, she would gobble it all up in record-breaking time and then be looking at me with her big brown eyes clearly pleading for seconds like Oliver Twist.

I'm not exaggerating. She would eat four times as much as other dogs.

It felt extreme, yet also it felt like this wasn't greed, she really did need the food. My instinct was that I shouldn't deny her, her hunger seemed so urgent. I didn't know much about dogs in these early days, but I could see her teats were quite swollen, a sign that a dog has recently given birth to puppies.

Now I've learned a lot more about animals, I would be able to tell you that she was breastfeeding by looking at her, but I wasn't really very knowledgeable then. There was never any sign of her babies though, I asked around and none of the locals or other volunteers had ever spotted them. We tried to follow her back through the jungle one time to see if we could find them and help them, but none could be found.

What often happens, as I learned from speaking to locals, is that new mummy dogs are dumped when they've had babies. It's not uncommon for them to poison the pups and dump the mum out in the jungle to fend for herself.

We worked on this assumption, that poor Beyoncé's little ones had met an untimely end and here she was alone, trying to survive. Of course I felt sorry for her, how miserable and cruel to lose your babies and get dumped out here by yourself? I soon built up a genuine rapport with her. Just as Lucky recognised me, street-smart

Beyoncé too would know the noise of the moped and come running out for a meal.

I was determined to boost her weight so I was bringing her the relatively expensive tinned meat at that stage. Whereas a regular, hungry street dog would polish off one tin and be sated (their bellies aren't that big as they're so used to eating sporadically) Beyoncé, I swear to god, was wolfing down four tins. I physically couldn't carry enough tins for her.

Jesus, what is wrong with this starving dog?

After she'd wolfed down the meals she would run straight off again.

One of my friends thought she had seen some puppies, but eight weeks passed by with this same, ravenous routine of Beyoncé's and no sign of any offspring.

One day she appeared and had clearly been attacked by another dog. She had quite a severe wound on her leg, something had clearly taken a decent bite out of Beyoncé.

She was the first street dog I felt confident enough to have a go at patching up myself. I cleaned her wound and sterilised it and fed her some basic antibiotics. It felt like a big step, patching her up by the side of the road, but I was able to heal her, and that felt like a real achievement and I was thrilled she trusted me. 'Thank you for making me better, Niall,' she seemed to be saying with those soulful big eyes. Then she hastily scampered off again.

It was a few days later, in July, when my friend Lana and I were making a fun video about feeding the dogs a nice special dinner (I try to keep the posts regular and keep the flow of vital donations coming in) when I turned around and standing behind me was Beyoncé … and her six little puppies! I couldn't believe it – they did exist, and they hadn't been poisoned. Beyoncé, like the incredible, protective mummy she was, had been keeping them safely hidden in a little den of an abandoned shack. Sensing the world was a dangerous place for unwanted pups, she'd kept her family out of sight.

We asked the vets what might have been happening, and their theory was that all those times Beyoncé had been hoovering up an insane amount of food, she was going straight back to the babies, regurgitating it all, and allowing them to eat it to survive. She'd also kept them alive and well by breastfeeding them too. No wonder there was nothing left of her. She had literally sacrificed everything she had to keep them all going, even if it meant nearly starving herself in the process.

I was blown away by her strength and the power of her maternal instinct. We cried out in delight when seeing these almost identical six pups come trotting happily behind their mum. All with the most adorable caramel-coloured fur with dark snouts – Beyoncé's cutest Mini-Me's. They were about 12 weeks old and all surprisingly strong and healthy.

Of course their ears were terribly infested with ticks, there were hundreds of them, and fleas, but this could be sorted out. Beyoncé had done all the hard work herself by keeping them protected, alive and thriving. They didn't even seem in the slightest bit malnourished.

Standing proudly by the side of the road with her six little pups in tow, the whole family were making their entrance into public life. Beyoncé seemed pleased with herself, the protective mummy. It was a real win that she trusted me now to show me her precious treasures.

Before I started this mission, I had no idea how in awe of a street dog I could be. But the love and sheer strength Beyoncé had shown, keeping her pups alive all by herself for those first three months of their lives, made me want to cry. I felt so honoured that she now trusted me to ask for my help with the next part. It really was as if she was saying to me, while looking at me with those wide eyes, 'I've got them this far, Niall, please can you help me with the next bit?'

And of course it was my absolute privilege to step in and lend a hand to this brave mummy and her much-beloved babies. The first thing I did was get them all cleaned up. I'd learned by now how to remove the ticks from the ears with medicine that clears them all up within 24 hours. I covered them all with flea powder, which makes the fleas hop off in horror, and I gave them all a good wash and dog shampoo.

Outside the family home where my mum, dad and I lived. I remember those being happy days, when I was oblivious that my world was about to be shattered.

I always loved being around animals. I begged my grandfather and uncles to take me with them when they went fishing.

Growing up I was obsessed with the outdoors and football – anything to get out of doing schoolwork and keep my overactive imagination stimulated.

LEFT: With a group of puppies I rescued from under a building in the jungle with my friends Rod and Jewells. Their lives are so delicate and precious. They all survived.

ABOVE: About a month after I started feeding the dogs, a newspaper called asking to do a story. They needed photos, and a friend took these with Daisy and Buttons, who are two of the first street dogs I fed.

LEFT: Rescuing Britney's puppies and keeping a keen eye on her, as she was still trying to protect them and violently attack me at this stage.

RIGHT: Derek, on the day he came into my care. He was utterly broken and only hours away from death. I presumed it would just be a case of giving him a good send-off, but he has proved me totally wrong.

Smiling with King Whacker a week after someone had tried to kill him with a pickaxe. We are both happy here, as we know he is going to survive.

A friend caught me collapsed in the wheelbarrow, utterly exhausted both mentally and physically from a day with the dogs. The toll it takes can be immense at times.

Distinguished Giuseppe. We took him off the streets to give him three months of care and a wonderful, graceful end to his life.

I don't get lots of time to relax, but when I do I'll pick a dog for 10 minutes' rest in the hammock. Just swaying and knowing that we should both be dead, we're in pure bliss.

RIGHT: McMuffin on her first visit to the vet after we scooped her up. She looked, smelled and acted as if it was the end of her life. McMuffin went on to beat cancer and be the mascot of the entire project.

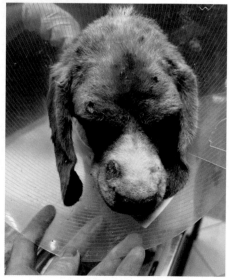

LEFT: The day McMuffin 'told' us she was ready to live. She was wearing yellow and red bandages to hide her cancerous tumours, so I looked on the McDonald's menu and found the name McMuffin. Perfect.

Lucky and Chopper were the first two dogs who captured everyone's hearts and imaginations. I loved them dearly, took them to the beach and made excuses to go and see them often. Then they just vanished.

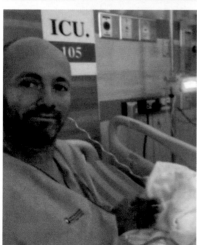

The day after I arrived in ICU. Sitting in that bed about to die, I decided that, if I did survive, I would change my entire life and do something with real purpose.

With Tina, who was a breeding dog tied to a short chain in agony. This is early in her recovery, but she had already become my shadow. We are both delirious with happiness and love in this photo.

A special day out at the beach for supermum Beyoncé and her little boy Ryan Gosling. After suffering so much pain in the jungle and being so brave, she deserved a special treat.

Marlon Brando was a sweet old gentleman. I fed him daily and cleaned his eyes for him. When he got hit by a car and was left in the middle of the road it was important to give him a big send-off with dignity.

I wasn't sure if little Rodney would make it, but this was one of the first photos where he had started to perk up and show that he had a future.

On my travels I'm always scooping up puppies that have been dumped. I've mastered being able to carry three safely in one hand while driving the bike with the other hand – needs must in an emergency.

I like to give the dogs little treats every so often – like making all 80 of them a full Christmas roast dinner with all the trimmings.

I feel completely free and at ease when out on my bike finding and saving dogs. I don't need possessions, a fancy car or any perks. Every second of the day feels rewarding, no matter how challenging it is.

Britney was the toughest rescue of all. She has gone from attacking people and other dogs to being a much calmer dog. She is a lot of work, but here she is in her very favourite place.

Snoop, Jumbo and Britney are my three dogs who live with me full time – all rescues who need extra-special care. They are always there waiting for me when I get home tired, looking for an adventure of their own!

Snoop getting out of his travel crate the day we arrived in Thailand. We hadn't seen each other for 24 hours and I had been sick with worry. Our bond is just pure love through thick and thin.

Beyoncé brought them all out for meal times now she realised they would be safe, and soon her own weight began to increase, as did her pups'. I imagine it was a bit nicer for them than regurgitated food from poor mum's tum!

I got them vaccinated, to avoid them catching all sorts of illnesses, and as soon as they were old enough I was able to have each one sterilised. It cost about $500, but it was worth it to give them a proper future. The cutest thing in the world was taking each of them to the vet to be neutered. Beyoncé would watch me beadily putting on their collars and taking them in. I would set off in the morning taking two at a time, and when I brought them home at five in the evening, once the vet had done the procedure, Beyoncé was always dutifully waiting by the roadside for me to return to her. She would lick them to welcome them home and fuss over them to check they were OK. This was a dog who was literally obsessed with her pups' welfare, and she totally trusted me with them. Patiently waiting for the jeep to return, she knew I would bring them home to her.

I adored each and every one of them. Two of them remained just Beyoncé's babies, three of them were named after vacuum cleaners – Hoover, Henry and Dyson – because they'd suck up whatever you put in front of them, and the prettiest little boy was named Ryan Gosling. I'd honestly never seen a more handsome lad in my life, and in his bright orange collar he just exuded all the star quality of a Hollywood heart-throb.

They are the loveliest little pack now. Brought up by their doting mum, they've all got the nicest manners you can imagine a street dog to have, they share their food nicely, they're respectful, and never snap at each other. Beyoncé had raised them impeccably.

I don't worry about this lot enduring lives on the streets. Every time I see their healthy, happy little gang, I know that by successfully having vaccinated and neutered them all, including Beyoncé herself, I've stopped maybe thirty to forty other puppies from being born and having to fight for survival on the streets. They look in good shape, as good as proper pets do. Thanks to their loving mum, and a little hand from me, they'd beaten the odds.

It was a real achievement, and super mum Beyoncé's behaviour and character made my heart overflow with so much love and respect for all the selfless mums in the world. I take my hat off to them all.

ELEVEN

NOT ALL DOGS ARE EASY TO LOVE

Britney is easily the toughest rescue I have ever done. I'm not just talking about the initial part, which was an experience that dialled my anxiety up to the max, but the whole time she has been with me. She's pushed me to the brink many times. Some days I swear at her, some days I have to chase her all over the country, and every day I have to give her patience and time that I struggle to find.

But I know that she learned her challenging behaviours as a reaction to terrible abuse in her early life. That is why every day I've been trying to show Britney that not everything in the world is a threat. It's also why she is named after Britney Spears, whose behaviour over the years has shown the scars of being manipulated and badly treated by people close to her.

I genuinely never knew how much I would be able to help Britney, so now when I see her play and interact with other dogs, I allow myself to feel a little bit proud and to think that maybe that's all down to me. It's been a tough old journey to get here so I'll talk you through it from the beginning …

Britney came from the most precarious and horrible situation I've encountered since I started doing this. I initially got a call from Terri, who does great work feeding dogs in the jungle. Terri had stumbled upon a female dog who had been dumped along with five puppies. She had approached the mum – who I would later name Britney – and the dog had lashed out and bitten her, so she called me to see what I could do. I drove up into the middle of the jungle and what greeted me was equal parts heartbreaking and terrifying.

Britney was built like a pit bull, with black and tan fur dappled with white covering her muscular body and a padlock and chain bolted around her neck – I suspect because she was a fighting dog they kept her on a short chain. Her eyes narrowed at me, distrusting what I might do to her. They flashed angrily if I got too close to her babies.

The puppies all looked like little terriers and wore sleek coats which were a mix of white, black and brown. They came out running to meet me, yelping away and seemingly keen to get acquainted, but as soon as I got up close to Britney, she charged us with eyes ablaze with aggression, her teeth bared, saliva dripping, ready to attack. After a few moments, I figured out that maybe if I had a long stick, I could keep Britney at bay and get through to the puppies to leave them some water and food.

I hated the idea of wielding a stick at an animal, it felt instinctively wrong, and I wouldn't have used it in any way other than for self-defence, but I couldn't think of a better way to be able to approach her. And every signal was crystal clear – this fiercely protective mummy would certainly take a hefty chunk out of anyone harming her babies.

With my stick in hand, just in case, I went back a few times on that first day to feed all of them and try and gain their trust. It was clear gaining Britney's trust, or remotely winning her over, was not going to be at all easy; she was still going for me, growling and snarling and flashing her fangs, even though I had the stick to protect myself. There I was, hopping about like I was doing an insane cross between break dancing and Morris dancing as she snapped viciously away at me.

I imagine it would have been quite a comical sight had I not been genuinely fearing for my limbs. I don't like to think about what might have happened if I didn't have the stick, and I had to brandish it pretty actively in her direction a few times to protect myself. However, as I did slowly inch closer, it became clear that the puppies were in big trouble. Each of the youngsters' ears were filled with dozens and dozens of parasitic ticks. Fattened up on the poor puppies' blood, the ticks looked like tiny shiny pebbles stuck hard onto their fur. Looking more closely, I could see it wasn't just the ears; their bodies were covered in ticks and these foul parasites filled the spaces in between their toes too. This sent things from bad to worse in my head. Now I knew the dogs were suffering and in pain, I fclt that if I was really committed to working with dogs in Thailand, I needed to find a way past Britney and help them.

Over the next few days, my friend Lana and I came up with a system to isolate the puppies from Britney one by one, get them up into the back of the jeep, and get some medicine into them to treat the ticks. We were literally sheltering there in the back of the jeep like it was some kind of fortress, as it was the only way we could ensure Britney wouldn't attack us. It felt like a dangerous thing to do; Britney clearly hadn't started to trust us at all yet and she still looked like she would gladly sink her sharp teeth into us at any available opportunity, but the puppies were so sick that we had to do it.

When Lana and I each had a puppy, I was able to administer a little bit of medicine to them, and clean them up with some special powder. The medicine started to work within 24 hours, I could see that the ticks had started to drop off, and that felt like a good victory. I also got my hands on some flea tablets for Britney. I really wanted to get them into her and make her feel better too, but if I just flung them over to her, there was a real possibility that the puppies would eat them and this could make them seriously ill. So I had to slowly isolate Britney away from the pack and thankfully luck was on our side that day, or perhaps she was just starving, but she mercifully gobbled the tablets.

Having given them some care and fed them over four to five days felt like real progress, but I knew they were on public land close to some houses which meant there was a genuine chance that locals would see them as a nuisance or a danger, and poison, shoot or kill them in some other way. This isn't me being dramatic, this unfortunately happens a lot, especially with dogs this aggressive. What's more, the pack had taken up residence underneath a JCB digger and all I could think of was that pretty soon somebody was going to need that digger, and get rid of the dogs so they could use it, either by scaring them off, or something much worse. I knew I had to move them somehow. I knew I had to catch Britney, but at that time I just didn't know how.

I was bringing Britney and the puppies food pretty frequently and keeping an eye on them. Sometimes I felt like I was moving closer and closer to the family but anytime I chose to try to catch them so as to move them away from this precarious place, Britney would try and bite me.

I knew my window to rescue them was closing, so I found myself a box and a dog-catching pole. These are basically like large nets hooped around a wide opening, like a kind of long-handled fishing pole, and I prepared to make a start. I had a lot of failed attempts. It was almost like some kind of montage sequence in a movie, and 'If at first you don't succeed …' was playing on a loop in my head. The rain was relentless at that point. When it rains here, it really chucks it down with torrential force. My clothes were sopping. I made more and more fruitless attempts and became wetter and wetter, but I never stopped trying to plot how I could catch a few of the puppies, then keep them somewhere, and then trap the others too.

After a lot of planning and difficulty, I managed to corner the six of them into an area in the jungle where there was a steep slope and I felt they wouldn't be able to make a run for it. I had decided that I needed to catch the five puppies first and isolate them away from Britney, then her ferocious maternal instincts would kick in and she might be more likely to come with me quietly (or so I hoped).

With great difficulty, I eventually caught all five puppies and put them in the box where I made sure Britney could see them and know that they were safe. Her reaction was fascinating to observe: for all that she was a pretty terrifying dog, she wouldn't leave her puppies. And for all that she was a caring mum, she still wasn't coming quietly to join them.

Therefore, I pulled on some welder's gloves, which she hopefully wasn't going to be able to bite through, found myself a long blue pole, which I hoped wasn't going to shatter in her jaws, and cornered her. It took me about an hour to finally catch her. I felt like some kind of modern-day cowboy, wrangling her towards the safety of the box. She squirmed, tried to bite through the pole, tried to go for me, tried to make a run for it, everything. But here we finally were with six potentially safe dogs.

If I'd had an ounce of energy left I would have lain down and sobbed from the relief and adrenaline coursing out of me.

When I think about that time now, I was probably pushing myself too hard. I was wound up like the tightest spring imaginable, and every single warning signal was flashing red in my mind.

Prior to the rescue, I couldn't sleep for days, as I thought about the puppies in the jungle, their mum trying to bite me, and locals trying to poison them. At the same time, I was looking to keep the show on the road with the other dogs that I look after, all while the pissing rain lashed down on all of us. In the old days I would have started with a six-pack of beer to 'calm down' and ended up on a four-day bender taking Valium and wine at 6 am to get back to 'normal'. Now I know the signs and some of the right things to do. I get offline. I exercise. I get massages. I eat well and do some breathing exercises. I tell people I'm struggling and take time off to look after myself. And I really need to be firm with myself and do these things without feeling that I'm letting the dogs down.

So suffice to say, I was just so relieved to catch her, get her into the box and pack her and the puppies off to the vet straight away. Although the medicine I'd given the puppies for the ticks had started to work, they needed further treatment with antibiotics, some cleaning, some vaccinations and some basic nourishment. With all this we were quickly able to get the puppies into good shape, and I felt confident enough to even name them: Caramel, Mocha, Latte, Americano and Frappuccino. (I do love my coffee!)

When we were able to get Britney out of the box at the vet's, I used a pair of bolt cutters to slice the padlock off from around her neck. It felt amazing to free her of this ugly hindrance, both physically and symbolically. I felt like I had released the weight of the world from her shoulders. She twisted her neck happily as if not believing she was lighter, and by removing this from her body, it was like her attitude to me changed too. Her dark eyes were ever so slightly less wary, she held herself a tiny bit less defensively. To this day, Britney's attitude hasn't changed towards many other people, she's still hyper suspicious of humans, but with me she did relax. She finally understood she was safe in my company, and crucially she didn't try to kill me anymore! The stick was put down and was never needed again, with me at least. I genuinely believe she was able to realise that I was her friend and saviour and she could calm down and relax.

★   ★   ★

After they had spent a period of recuperation at the vet's, I wanted Britney and her family to have a safe and quiet place to grow and start a new life. So we found them a really remote part of the jungle, away from people and cars and other canines, ensconced them happily there, and built up more trust with them. One of the key ways I did this was by building them a little wooden house with a cushioned platform for sleeping, and a corrugated iron roof to keep the rain off. They stayed there for about a week with good access to food and water, and Britney especially was really starting to come out of her shell and relax. She seemed to feel her babies were safe and she could lower her own barriers.

So it was a real kick in the teeth for us when, unfortunately, one day I came to replenish their food and found that their little house and shelter had been smashed to pieces. Their water and food bowls had been taken away. The dogs were fine, thankfully. But the message seemed very clear: Get these dogs out of here … I don't know who it was who smashed the shelter, but I immediately thought, 'OK, these dogs have to be moved straight away.' We hadn't gone through all that together for them to come to any harm now.

Sadly, this wasn't the first time I had experienced animosity from some locals. Not everyone loves dogs and animals, and there are a core group of people who would want to see street dogs extinct. Since I've been working with the dogs and have begun this whole mission to improve their lives, I have realised there are some people who aren't happy about it. There are many around the island who think I am a certified crazy person. The Irish nutter who's come to the island and has gone mad.

I would say half of them are entirely indifferent to what I am doing with the dogs. And there is another 20 per cent who seem to like the fact I'm dog mad; they smile at me and give me the thumbs up when they pass, or they come and chat and watch the feeding rounds and interact with the dogs. Funnily enough, it's often the people who have so little in life, like the migrant workers, who are the kindest towards the dogs and bring them their scraps.

But there are certainly 30 per cent, I'd estimate, who seem to hate me being here. And I can understand why. Of course I can. The dogs are attracted to food. And so if I'm putting food out near their house, the dogs will all congregate there to enjoy a meal. Would I want a dozen dogs starting to hang around the home, fighting, barking and shitting all over the place? I can totally see their point of view. I try to be respectful and not put food too close to houses as I realise that's unfair.

Since I've been doing this I've been sworn at, and swerved at on the road, I've had cars come very close to me and drive very fast in threatening ways. I feel like that's a warning, a menacing signal: 'Leave the dogs alone, you crazy Westerner, and get out of our neighbourhood, you're not welcome here,' is how I'd roughly translate it.

It's often the wealthier people who are the most anti-dog and don't want them near their properties. I had a woman one day screaming at me. Her house was like a mansion compared to most locals out here. And my presence – and the dogs' – was unwelcome. Shouting at me in a mixture of English and Thai, I could get the drift of what she was saying. 'Barking … shitting everywhere … I don't want these dogs!' She was hysterically angry and shaking. I apologised and promised to steer clear in the future.

I even had a guy pull a knife on me one time. It wasn't like a street crime-style knife threat you might get in the city, like a mugging or something, I didn't feel in immediate danger. Lots of people here carry knives for chopping coconuts and the like, or use machetes and things like that to do their work in the jungle. So seeing men with knives is not something so remarkable. But this guy got really angry and stood 15 metres away from me while I was feeding one day, furiously waving the weapon at me in a 'back-off' motion. I never felt he was going to actually try and use it, thank God. But it was a sure signal: 'Stop feeding the dogs, you fucking foreigner.'

I've never been an aggressive person. I'm very much into keeping the peace in life, thank you very much. The best thing I can do is simply to smile at everyone. I bow my head, or I hold my hands up, signalling that I mean no harm.

I always try to be respectful towards everyone, however much animosity they can show, because it is their country after all, and it's a different culture and I totally get that. I'm lucky to be living here and the very last thing I want to do is bring trouble to the island I love. But it was disheartening to see someone had purposefully smashed up the shelter we had made for Britney. And I feared it would be a setback for the progress we had so painstakingly made with her.

I rallied some of my friends to help me out. I am so grateful I have people, fellow animal lovers, to call on like this. We checked Britney into another vet. She was still quite aggressive and unsettled with people so they put her in a steel crate, and we used this to give her a good health check-up including some blood tests, treatment for para-sites and, of course, we made sure she had that all-important sterilisation. The idea of any more little Britneys coming into the world was frankly terrifying.

With Britney off having her treatment, I felt like I needed to hurry up and find homes for the puppies. I put them up on social media and, truthfully, I was hoping for a bit of a miracle. But they *can* happen: Frappuccino was quickly adopted to a forever home with a lovely Thai woman called Grace. This made him the ninth dog I had managed to re-home since starting this work. I wasn't surprised he was snapped up quickly as he looked like a lovely small terrier with a white body and big black splotches like a mini Friesian cow.

Amazingly, people popped up in Bangkok offering to take the remaining four puppies, but only if I could get them there the next day. Bangkok is about a thousand kilometres away from where I live, about the distance from London to Edinburgh and back, so I had to pay for a private taxi bus and pack the four of them into the back with toys and blankets and snacks. I kissed them all goodbye, but felt so happy they could all get to a wonderful new and loving home in the big city. All five of them, Caramel, Mocha, Latte, Americano and Frappuccino are doing great to this day: they've all been sterilised and are fully recovered from the ticks and their other illnesses. So we have to give Britney the credit for keeping them alive, despite how stress inducing it had all been.

Now I was just left with Britney in the vet's. Still nobody could get near her. The team at the vet's were having to take her out of her crate with a funny plastic cone on her head so she wouldn't bite anyone. But good old Britney would have gladly tried to if she could. I clearly couldn't ask anyone else to give a home to a dog who was this disturbed and, clearly, dangerous. I felt it wouldn't end well for anyone if she was left in the jungle either. So the options were limited. Because she trusted me, there was no other choice really but to take her home to live with me.

I tentatively introduced her to Snoop and Jumbo back at my place. Shockingly, she attacked Snoop straight away.

Snoop is no alpha dog, he's aged and vulnerable, so it felt like an unprovoked attack on a weaker animal. Not for the first or last time, I was annoyed with Britney.

This was a huge setback. I had given her a tiny bit of trust, and she'd abused it. I realised that she was probably just going to be jealous of anyone who came close to me, but I thought to myself, 'I can't keep this dog.'

I kept them separate that night but went to bed anxious.

People were incredibly supportive and encouraging, telling me to stick with it and that it would be easier soon. I'm not sure five months counts as 'soon', but I think that is how long it took for Britney to really feel at home.

She definitely began to calm down after two or three months, but I had to keep her on a lead in the house for a while as she learned to live side by side with the other dogs and me. As time has gone on, I've realised just how damaged Britney is. Her aggression, the padlock, her stocky build and behaviours make me think she must have been used in dog fights before she was dumped in the jungle.

I guess therefore that it's not surprising that there is so much trauma in her. These days I think about 90 per cent of that trauma has gone, but I can't see that we will ever manage to process the rest of it with her. Although she trusts other dogs a little bit now and goes off to play with some of them, she's still always liable to turn around and snap. She hasn't really made any progress with other humans at all. I've tried slowly introducing her to volunteers but she still snarls and barks at them and nips at their legs. She's the one dog people dread dealing with and who can blame them?

This means I'm the only one who can handle her, and she's so energetic that it's a daily slog to take her up and down the hills to get her tired enough that she'll calm down for the evening.

With all of this responsibility for Britney solely on me, there are definitely days when I break. There are days where I'm in the middle of the jungle and I just lose it because of her anti-social, aggressive behaviour. There are days when I feel like I have given all my emotional energy to a sick or dying dog that I'm caring for, but then I have to find more because Britney is acting up or flying off to who knows where. Sometimes she will have been perfect for a few days, so I trust her and don't watch her as much as I should, and then she'll suddenly run off from me or she'll dive into the jungle and not come back, or try to attack something.

Sometimes these things are just tiring or exasperating. We might be on the moped and she'll jump off and try to go for a cat and then I worry that's dangerous for me, her and other people. I have certainly had a few Britney-related injuries too, mostly when we are walking peacefully or maybe I have had a long day and have therefore let my guard down. Then someone will pass on a moped or a dog will get her hackles up and she will just launch herself and she'll nearly dislocate my shoulder or jar my back.

I would guess that Britney is still only two or three years old so she's still a puppy really, and I hope she might mellow with age. What's more, I know that dogs are not born like this. They learn this behaviour from somewhere. They are abused, either by an owner or by a group of people. I really hope that we can maybe work on her a bit more with humans, but I think the lesson that I have learned with her is that changing behaviours and how animals react to situations takes a very long time and a lot of effort. I know this is true for humans too, both from my own personal experience and from seeing others try and process trauma over the years.

A lot of people are immensely damaged. Maybe from what happened to them in childhood, or from when they were young adults or from what other people have inflicted on them. Sometimes people can get into therapy and unlearn damaging reactions or thoughts and get better and be better. But sometimes the abuse and the suffering people have endured or been through is just so severe that there is always a residual hurt. A kernel of pain that just can't be cracked or washed out of the system. I think with Britney we might not be able to unlearn or change all her problematic behaviours, but I have been her little lucky break and given her a chance in life. She has found one person who will look out for her and be on her side and support her to make a change.

Now that I have looked after Britney for so long I almost feel like a parent guiding a difficult child through life. Although I don't have kids, I know that raising them isn't all birthday cakes and high fives. I know parents have moments where they can lose it with their children and then regret it terribly afterwards, and there have been times where I've stood there shouting 'Fuck you Britney! I hate you!' in a jungle clearing when I don't know where she has gone.

I know that's not right, but also I know that that's life. Sometimes it is the people who you care about the most who break you the easiest. I think we are all bad at admitting this: we pretend things are all sweetness and light and all emotional journeys are helpful and linear. But they're not. They're long and painful and they stop and start, and take unhelpful turns. I feel strongly that it is important to share this. I know this journey has been much harder for Britney, but I also know deep down that she is a good dog now. Despite everything, I love her dearly.

TWELVE

THE
FEISTY CANCER
SURVIVOR

McMuffin is simply one of the finest dogs you'll ever meet. A queen of canines, she's such an important part of everything I want to achieve and she has such a big impact on people who know and love her (everybody loves her, once they've met her, and I know you would too).

She came into my life at the tail end of August 2022, when I had one of the toughest days I'd yet experienced while working with the dogs. I'd been on the road with my Australian friend Rod, an ex-policeman who retired out here the year before I arrived. I've really leaned on him, and his partner Jewells too, for help since I've started this whole mission. They're both passionate dog lovers and now good friends, and we often go on rescues together.

This day, at the end of summer, it was slightly overcast. In Koh Samui there's a 20 per cent chance of a hot sunny day at this time of year, and an 80 per cent chance of some clouds. This was an overcast day with a splattering of rain, and we'd picked up several sick dogs. We'd been taking twenty-odd puppies for vaccinations and were caring for a dog we'd called Bender (because his poor leg was bent, and not because he resembled someone who'd been on a big one). In fact, his leg was badly busted. We were trying to catch him and put him in a box to take him off for an X-ray. He'd likely need an amputation, not ideal, but he'd then be OK and wouldn't have to live with the pain and medication.

It had been a particularly gruelling day, I was feeling beaten and keen to get home for the evening, picking up a Pad Thai for dinner on the way. (You would never guess I used to be a chef, as I eat mainly takeaways these days. I'd rather use my time for cooking for the dogs than myself.) So there I was, just about to climb back into Rod's truck when a little Thai man approached me from the other side of the road.

He seemed extremely sheepish as he walked over towards me. He looked a little down on his luck, to be frank. He was pretty dishevelled, his clothes had seen better days, and my first impression was that he was a homeless man. I even wondered if he was maybe a drunk (not that I was judging that, I felt grateful for the millionth time that I was eighteen months sober up to that point). But I wondered if he was looking for money or something from me. While I didn't ever beg on the street when I needed a drink, I could relate to the urge above all other urges to source alcohol when I was in the grip of my own addiction.

The poor guy didn't have a word of English, and my Thai was limited, but he wiggled his fingers at me, beckoning me to follow him.

Jesus, what the hell is this? A scam?

In all honesty, I was uneasy about where this was going. But there was something in the guy's manner that made me trust him enough to go and see what he was trying to show me.

So following him out the back, he led me to a kind of allotment area, where there were some plants and flowers. It was quite run-down. I realised this was where he lived. I could tell he was a bit 'simple', for want of a better word (though I'm sure that's not very PC of me to say!). He wasn't drunk as I had first thought, yet he certainly seemed to have some kind of mental impairment. I felt it would have been mean to walk away from him.

It's been a long day, but have some tolerance, Niall. Be nice.

Out the back, there was a tatty old blue cage, with the door open, so I peered inside … bracing myself to find some horrible case of animal cruelty. By then I'd got a sort of reputation among locals (as well as ex-pats and tourists) for being the person to call when a dog was in trouble. The mad Irish guy who's obsessed with dogs, is probably how I was seen.

Yet instead of some poor abused dog what I found was a truly miserable-looking soul with a makeshift collar, in the form of a worn piece of rope, around its neck. It was a beagle, not one of the usual mixed breeds you come across here.

This was certainly less common, but not totally unheard of in Thailand. Occasionally people here buy an expensive pedigree dog – like this one in front of me – but then can't afford to pay the vet bills when they get sick. And because they're often bred so unethically, with the mummy dogs treated as cash cows, illnesses like canine parvovirus can be more common. But many breeders of expensive pedigree dogs don't have the welfare of the puppies first and foremost. Their greed comes before the pups' health.

And the people who have paid lots of baht for a dog, once it gets sick, rather than trying to get the pet sorted out and made better, instead ditch it on the streets and leave it to fend for itself and inevitably die a lonely and painful death. It's utterly heartbreaking and miserable how these dogs can be treated.

I had no idea what the background was of this unfortunate beagle, but I suspected this might be the story for this one too. A female, of about seven to eight years old, she was one of the most pathetic and upsetting sights I'd ever seen in my entire life.

She looked half dead, with all these weird boil-looking things over her entire body, most of them oozing pus. When I counted them, there were over forty taking over her body. She was also – of course, like they all are – ridden with fleas, and covered in hundreds and hundreds of blood-sucking ticks. She looked at death's door: head down, quivering body, eyes clouded over, her spirit completely broken. *Christ almighty.*

I had to know what had happened, or as much as I possibly could. So I immediately rang a Thai friend, Phleng. She was my go-to translator on speed dial when I needed it, and this was one of the times I knew I had to phone her. I asked Phleng if she would help me out by speaking to this man, and finding out what was going on, and then translate it all back to me in English.

While they jabbered away in Thai for several minutes, him doing his best to explain how he came to have the beagle in his funny backyard area, I stared at her. *She can't have much longer.* I didn't fancy her chances of even surviving a ride to the vet's in all honesty. But I couldn't leave her to die here. She opened her eyes and we looked at each other. 'You poor baby,' I whispered. 'Let's see what we can do for you, make you more comfortable at least.'

I thought of Tyson, and holding him as he drew his last breath months before. I thought of the other dogs and pups I'd seen pass. She didn't seem in much better shape. She looked far worse in fact, thanks to the hideous looking, boil-like things covering her whole body.

With the phone call ended, the Thai man handed me back my mobile. He didn't seem to even know how to use it properly or where to speak into it. Phleng told me what she'd been able to find out from their chat.

It turned out the poor Thai man had been doing his best to keep the beagle alive. He hadn't really got a clue, bless him. Why would he? I was new to all this too.

He had been feeding her a little rice and a little water, and had been trying to douse her in flea powder, which had probably irritated the boil-like things even more. He was trying his best, explained Phleng to me on the phone, with what very little he had.

I felt guilty I'd thought he was a drunk. He was clearly born with many challenges in life and I realised his sheepish way of approaching me was shyness, and it had taken a lot of courage to come and ask a foreigner for help.

It turned out that the dog had been dumped quite some time ago. The man obviously had no money, but his instinct was to care for the dog, and fair play to him, he'd kept the dog alive. She would have died weeks earlier had no one fed her or offered her water. I think even the affection and basic care he'd shown her would have made a difference. Dogs are like humans in that way, and if they're abandoned and ill they might give up the will to live a little earlier than if there is some hope that someone will love them. In my experience dogs are mainly optimistic souls.

The Thai man obviously saw me as somebody who could maybe try to help him, and help the desperately sick beagle. So he'd plucked up the courage to approach me, which can't have been easy for someone with all his issues, mustering up all his confidence to get me to follow him and show me the thing he hadn't told anyone else about. He'd done it for the dog's sake. My heart went out to him.

Dog lovers come in all shapes and sizes, but we recognise that strong bond we all share when we see it.

Truthfully, at that moment, I didn't have much of a plan for this poor beagle, but I scooped her up and headed to the truck anyway.

'Mate, you're not going to believe what I've found,' I warned Rod, as I carried her small, poorly body in my arms, trying to avert my eyes from the yellow pus of the boils and filthy ticks crawling into them.

Rod's face was a picture of horror when he saw the state of her. You'd certainly have to be a true dog lover to even let her in your car to be honest. But luckily, Rod is. And so we loaded her carefully into the back, making her as comfortable as we could with some old towels and blankets, and Rod put his foot down as we drove straight to the vet's before closing time.

Well, I will never, ever forget the smell in the car coming off her. It was the vilest, most excruciating assault I've ever had on my nose. It was utterly rank. Putrid. Like rotting meat with rancid, fruity undertones. I don't even have the words to describe it. But for the first time since the pandemic had ended, I actually wished I had a face mask to put on me again. Rod, who'd had to deal with various dead bodies when he was a policeman, compared the smell of the beagle to the stench of weeks-old decomposing corpses. Which I hope for your sake you've never smelled, but let me assure you, this was vile.

While Rod sped as quickly as a man can over the muddy back roads of Koh Samui to reach the vet's, I wound the window right down and hung my head out, trying to gulp in fresh air so I wouldn't be sick in the car. Rod and I exchanged a look of 'what the fuck are we doing?' at the absurdity of the situation. Doing this work, you have to have a laugh even in the dark moments, or you'd cry all the time over the dogs' lives.

We weren't laughing, however, when the vet ushered us into the surgery. The vet was equally shocked by the state of the dog. She was in dire straits. Her blood tests came back and they were disastrous. They showed she was as close to death as possible. Her blood count was way, way below what it should have been. She had tick fever, blood parasites and anaemia. All of these things were about to kill her.

'She's hours from death, I'm afraid,' the vet warned us, shaking his head.

What the hell were all these oozing boil things on her though? I'd never seen them before on dogs. Even the ones in bad states didn't look, or smell, quite like this one.

For some reason, whether to save her or just understand what this was, I really wanted a second opinion on the beagle. So we decided to take her to another vet to have a look. I scooped her up, put her back into the car with the blankets, and Rod once again drove like a maniac to get us there. The prognosis wasn't much better.

'You could try a blood infusion,' the second vet suggested. 'It might help, but there's no guarantees.'

A blood transfusion would cost about $1,500. That is a lot of baht wages.

The beagle was hooked up to a drip and we all spent a long time cleaning her up. It was well beyond the surgery's closing time but we were allowed to sort her out. We painstakingly removed every single tick and flea from her body, anything to offer her a little more comfort and dignity, I thought, in what might be her final hours.

Then the vet suggested we leave her with him overnight and go away and 'have a think about it'. He was quite clearly using the vet language I interpreted to mean, 'It's the end of the road for this animal, get your affairs in order and have her put out of her misery.'

Making these decisions is so hard. If it was your beloved pet, it would be different. You'd automatically have a go at saving her with the expensive blood transfusion. You'd pay the cash and hope for the best outcome with the medical care you had at your disposal. But this wasn't a pet, this beagle was a street dog we'd literally picked up from the side of the road hours earlier.

It wasn't that I couldn't find the money, but I had to be sensible. I had to consider the cost of a blood transfusion (which may or may not work), and what else could be

achieved with that same amount of cash. You could sterilise many other dogs with the money, which would help
with the much bigger picture.

With the dilemma whirling round and round in our
heads, we left the beagle in the vet's overnight. Rod and I
discussed her endlessly, but I knew really what needed to
be done.

*Her time is up, Niall. Put the poor thing out of her misery
soon.*

Driving home with a heavy heart that night, I took a
detour to call in on the kind Thai man. He'd kept the dog
alive with his love and pathetically basic care, and he
deserved to know what was happening to her. I'm not sure
he'd ever watched a video on a phone before, but I handed
it over so he could see the vet explaining in Thai what the
beagle's problems were. His eyes welled up.

I spoke to the lady who owned the local shop, and she
told me that she let the man stay with her for free because
she felt so sorry for him and he had no one else. His only
source of income was selling fruit by the roadside, and she
said that every day once he'd sold what he had, he would
run off with his 100 baht (which is about two or three
dollars) and he'd spend it all buying dog food for the stray
dogs. He had neither the tools, nor the money or the
knowledge to fix the beagle, but he'd clearly tried his best.

By the time I arrived home, I felt worn down and very
low.

I'll have her put out of her misery tomorrow, I vowed. It wasn't fair on her, with all the health issues she was suffering, to try and prolong the agony anymore. If it hadn't been for the big-hearted Thai man she would surely have passed several weeks ago.

I thought of her deathly smell, the chronically bad blood results. There wasn't much point her carrying on.

I'd lost dogs before, of course. Tyson was the first, but there had been many more. That's part of the job, and you have to harden yourself to the loss. I try not to post the miserable news on my social media, no one wants to scroll through with their morning coffee and read all about dying dogs. But sadly, away from my social media feeds, this is what we often have to cope with.

It had been one of those days where you feel like you've been smacked around the face. I couldn't let myself fall into a depressive gloom right then, though. I needed to be strong and keep going.

One trick I've learned to ward off the blues is to muster every inch of positive thinking I can. And so I thought of the good things I'd achieved that day with Rod. We'd vaccinated twenty puppies against the parvovirus. We'd given Bender, with his busted leg, a better quality of life. The beagle would not die alone or without pain relief or someone giving her a chance.

I thought of the man in his shack, bowing his head to thank me for taking her to the vet's.

The answer in front of me was very clear. Yet I tossed and turned and eventually fell into an uneasy sleep around 4 am.

Next morning, after sorting out Snoop and doing my feeding rounds, I arrived at the vet's before opening-up time.

Steeling myself to be brave, I'd do the right thing and have the poor beagle put to sleep.

The vet confirmed that there had been no changes to her health overnight. I followed him through to where she was being kept, still on the drip.

She looked up at me. Big brown, soulful eyes. And I just spotted a tiny chink of spirit in them, in her. She wasn't ready to quit. Her fur already looked better than it did yesterday, thanks to the hours we'd put in removing the parasites. And she moved her paw an inch, as she looked at me, a tiny gesture as if to say, 'I'm still here. Give me a chance.'

I don't know what it was exactly, but something in me did a complete U-turn in that moment. I thanked the vet and paid for the tests she'd had. But I just couldn't bring myself to put this girl down.

'Come on you beautiful beagle, let's try one more time,' I said, scooping her up yet again, which she was getting used to now. 'Perhaps it will be third time lucky.'

The third vet was able to correctly diagnose that this dog had cancer. Which should have been obvious to me really all along. Those forty-odd boil-like things that were so disgusting were in actual fact, malignant tumours. The poor thing had a form of cancer called TVT, transmissible venereal tumour. It's spread between dogs and is sexually transmitted through direct skin-to-skin contact.

As horrible as it sounds however, this vet had seen cases of TVT before. And he had managed to treat them successfully. There was a reasonably good chance that this kind of cancer would respond well to chemotherapy treatment. My ears pricked up on hearing this news, and I could swear on my life the beagle's did too. Which isn't as mad as it sounds you know, because there is definite evidence that dogs are very adept at reading our faces for clues. So if she sees me perk up, she instinctively does too.

The vet said that providing we could get all the other issues that were currently threatening to kill her under control – the tick fever, anaemia and flea infestation – she might actually recover, if she was able to undergo chemo-therapy.

Holy shit! I grinned. *We're gonna give this girl a chance!*

My decision from the night before was wiped away in an instant. No one was pretending the future would not be hazardous for her. A street dog getting chemotherapy seemed like a crazy idea, I know. It would be long and painful, and expensive, with no guarantees that it would end well. But once I knew there was a tiny glimmer of hope, I just couldn't give up on her. There was simply something about this animal.

I stroked her gently, and could swear on my life that despite the discomfort she must have been in, I saw her crack a little smile at me.

The vet always warned me that the road to the beagle's recovery would be a long one. Cancer is a bastard, as so many of us have learned. It's the disease we all dread getting and the one that touches most of us at some stage of our lives, whether it's you or a loved one who gets diagnosed.

And it was no different for this dog. Her cancer was life threatening. In fact, she ended up staying at the vet's for two and a half months in total. That's how serious it was.

I visited her every day. And as soon as I saw her all dolled up in her bright yellow and red bandages, I immediately pointed at her and said, 'McDonald's!' She was wearing the exact hues of the fast-food chain which we couldn't help laughing about in the surgery.

What could we call her? We had registered her with the vet just as 'Beagle', but she deserved a proper name, fitting for the funny, brave little character she had quickly become.

Big Mac? McNuggets? French Fries?

I googled the restaurant menu for inspiration; nothing quite fitted, yet she couldn't just be 'the Beagle' anymore.

Right at the bottom of the list, I spotted 'McMuffin' and knew it was absolutely perfect for this sweet little survivor, peering out from the top of her bandages with a zest for life and wild optimism.

And didn't we all fall head over heels in love with McMuffin. All the staff at the vet's were instantly enchanted by her guts and smitten with her cheerful nature.

By looking at her teeth, the vet said she was probably seven years old, eight maximum. For the first three weeks, the focus was on treating her with antibiotics to fight off the immediate infections that were making her so poorly.

It would only be worth giving her chemotherapy to battle the cancer if she was well enough to survive. That was the number one priority. She was bandaged up and her bloods were frequently monitored. There were a lot of touch and go times. You might think it sounds silly to say a beagle looks pale, but she honestly did appear so white initially. She was desperately anaemic and had very deathly-white pale gums, which is a bad sign in dogs. Going to see her at the vet's every day reminded me exactly of visiting relatives on cancer wards; they just look a certain way. And so did McMuffin.

But the vet was pleased enough with her progress, her vital statistics were looking much better, and after three weeks, by September, McMuffin was well enough to proceed with the chemotherapy.

And I couldn't wait for the moment we began to fight the awful tumours. She was literally covered in them and they looked so sore and painful. They were on her face, on her nose. She had five around her arse, she had tumours between her paws. Just horrible.

Her innate star quality made her the celebrity of the surgery. McMuffin, clearly thrilled to be given another shot at life, would walk around like she owned the place, happily greeting everyone she crossed with a tail wag. 'Here I am!' she seemed to say, strutting around, cute as hell in her funny wardrobe of bandages. 'I'm McMuffin, the street dog with her own oncologist. Get me!'

It was impossible to think this was the same dog we'd found in the box so close to death. I posted pictures of her online and people all over the world instantly adored her as much as we all did. The best thing of all was seeing how her vivacious spirit was spreading hope, joy and inspiration to real-life people on the other side of the world who were also fighting cancer. I was suddenly getting so many messages on Instagram and Twitter from people who were themselves currently on cancer wards, undergoing chemo, awaiting surgery, or in remission. They wrote to me saying they had taken massive inspiration from McMuffin.

I never imagined the effect she would have on people, or that I'd be sent messages and pictures from hospital wards, from daughters with their mums saying they were following McMuffin's journey together, and looked forward to all the updates I posted.

She was one street dog but symbolised so much more. She's everything that's great about dogs.

Of course, it goes without saying that her vet bills were staggeringly high. Eye watering, to be honest. It ended up being about $5,000 in total to fix her. I couldn't have justified spending that amount on one dog if it meant many more would be losing out. It's like *Sophie's Choice*, a tough decision for any parent to have to choose between their children, and that would have felt wrong.

However, because McMuffin had so many fans by now, from all over the globe can you believe, that every time a vet bill was presented to me and I posted it online, the incredible community of animal lovers stepped in to help. I've honestly never seen anything like it. The bills were coming every three days, and each time some big-hearted person would volunteer to cover it. People were contributing $200, $500 and similar amounts in euros and pounds to pay for McMuffin's medical costs.

It blew my mind that people could be so kind and generous.

Deep down, I was slightly worried it would all be a waste of time; for the people who had so kindly paid her vet bills, I was terrified I'd be letting them down too. But she was inspiring so many people. It had become bigger than just a dog on the other side of the world with cancer now; it was like this little warrior had become a real beacon of hope.

Ever since I'd found McMuffin, I'd gone to bed at night visualising her in the little place I had been planning for so many months – the sanctuary where sick and needy dogs could stay until they'd either got back up on their feet or while they were waiting to be re-homed. The vet bills for McMuffin were partly so high because she needed somewhere safe and warm to stay while she was undergoing her treatment. So having her board at the vet's was an extra $30 a day. It's not hugely expensive, but it soon adds up. I was desperate to see her at this new place, which would also be providing shelter for so many others in need.

Very soon after I'd started the 10,000 dogs mission, it was apparent that I'd need a sanctuary of some kind. A safe, clean place with kennels for dogs, like a halfway house. It would be a little haven before dogs could, in my ideal world, be placed into their loving, caring forever homes. Or for those dogs who would always be happier on the streets, it would still be a place to come while they recovered from neutering operations and such like.

Now, after months of dreaming and planning, it was all finally taking shape.

Buying land to build kennels on was certainly a challenge. I needed somewhere quiet away from the roads and tourists. It's not really advertised online, so you have to find it through word of mouth, asking locals if they know of anywhere suitable, and asking on Facebook groups. I must have seen a hundred potential places, all beautiful spots and just what I needed, but as soon as I said it was to keep dogs there, people became wary. I think they were worried I would go off and leave the dogs and they'd be left to deal with them. You can see why they weren't keen.

So very luckily I eventually found a lovely old Thai woman who's an animal lover and was keen on the plans. She had about an acre, roughly half the size of a football pitch. There was nothing on it apart from jungle, so it would mean clearing it all out before anything could be built, but it was perfect. We needed some diggers, and we hired some manual labourers to help, as well as myself and the volunteers all rolling up our sleeves to get stuck in. We had to dig very deep to make a well for fresh water, and we used solar panels for the electricity.

I knew absolutely nothing about construction, but Rod had some experience with building villas so he was able to advise on structures and practical aspects. An amazing lady, Taay, from England, who had been so supportive on social media, had managed to raise an incredible £12,000 with her Girls Group (the GG as they're known), which I will always be so grateful for as we couldn't have done it without her. I put in the rest of the money myself as I firmly felt that anyone who was kind enough to make donations would want to see that money used directly for the dogs' medicines, food and sterilising.

We built some simple kennels to house ten dogs initially, but the plan was there would soon be double that. There was a small office and a place to safely store medicines. Snoop and Jumbo would come down to the land to inspect the progress every day, and it was basic but each little kennel had ventilation to keep the air coming in, and a little ramp up to a raised bed as dogs prefer to be higher up and feel safer than when they're just on the ground.

I really didn't want it to be clinical, like you imagine dog pounds are, slightly prison-like. I really wanted it to smell nice with fragrant plants and pretty flowers and painted walls, more like little personal suites rather than kennels (and that's what I call them!).

We had to create a gravel road for cars to come in, but we also built fun things to benefit the poorly dogs and puppies, like a little beach and a swimming pool. A proper little haven and safe place, it's even officially called Happy Doggo Land, which makes me smile.

The plan is to develop it more, and have a kitchen on site to make the food and have somewhere people can sit and drink coffee and meet the dogs.

That's the vision for it for the long term. But in the short term, I was absolutely over the moon to have the basics ready to welcome dogs.

* * *

After five weeks of chemo administered in the form of pills, McMuffin was showing signs of recovery. Her energy levels were improving by the day. I was able to start taking her for small walks, just 50 metres, then 100 metres, on the path outside the vet's initially, as she was so weak, but she loved the change of scenery and her little light-brown-and-white tail would be all waggy. She would pause to sniff at flowers and trees and seem inquisitive about the world around her, which was such a relief to witness.

I allowed myself to fantasise that she would still be with us at Christmas, perhaps in red and white bandages looking like Santa Claus. I wanted to get her out of the vet's surgery and safely at home with us.

As the chemo continued she would trot a little further each day, charming everyone whose path she crossed in her jaunty little bandages. Fans of McMuffin started sending in little cheerful accessories for her to wear. She just had the X factor, she was universally adored, and walking into the vet's it was like it had become McMuffin's practice. She'd trot in merrily and be the star of the show.

I know it's a terrible cliché about cancer when people say it's like fighting a battle. But for McMuffin it was just so true. Her warm brown eyes were alive with spirit and determination. She just had so much fight in her, a real little warrior. I beamed walking next to her.

On and on she battled. By October, after ten long weeks staying at the vet's, McMuffin had managed three weeks of her chemo (she needed ten in total in the end) and the tumours were fading. She was deemed well enough to be allowed to come to our little sanctuary.

I nearly exploded with happiness picking her up to drive her home. I had no idea whether McMuffin would know what balloons were, or if she'd like the stuffed toy I got her, but I felt she deserved a little surprise party in her new home.

Because her cancer is transmissible, McMuffin still had to stay away from the other dogs for a while. But if she carried on making progress I knew she'd love to make new friends as soon as she could. Sitting on the step with her and all the balloons that night, I shed a little tear of happiness. 'I'm a silly old softie, aren't I, my McMuffin?' I chuckled to her.

But she didn't see. She was pressed too closely into me and happily exhausted already from all the running around in her new home.

I had been regularly calling in on the Thai man who originally introduced me to McMuffin back in the summer. I supported him with food for his dogs and small amounts of money to boost his fruit-selling income.

He was always pleased to see me. I'd taken a video of McMuffin finally leaving the vet's but decided I didn't want to get his hopes up in case she took a turn for the worse. It was only after several more weeks and I felt confident we really had turned a corner and I could tell him a happy story that I showed him the video. I wasn't sure how much he would be taking in, but he recognised McMuffin and his whole face lit up. He immediately ran off like an excited child to tell the shopkeeper the good news, and she came out and rolled her eyes at me, and we all laughed together in delight about the happy turn of events. It made him so happy to see her looking so well. A moment of pure joy.

McMuffin still needed a lot of care, she still needed her bandages, and it was vital she was kept clean. She kept getting infections, as her immune system was so weakened by the chemo. But she'd pick herself up and carry on.

As soon as she was at the sanctuary, McMuffin developed into even more of an unbelievable character.

She's the little madam of the place, she's the queen. Never bossy, but she guides the other dogs in such a loving and caring way. She now acts as a therapy dog, helping those we have rescued over their traumas, such as Hope, who was abused with a nail gun and machete, and King Whacker, who someone attempted to brutally murder. More on them later!

McMuffin is into everyone's business all the time, checking in on their kennels. She's a little dynamo, badgering each and every dog she comes into contact with into happiness. She climbs on tables, she rolls around with puppies. She's just one of those souls who brings light into everyone's life.

Because of everything we have been through with

McMuffin, it's been hard knowing what the next steps for her should be. Originally of course, I was desperate to keep her in the sanctuary. But the aim of this mission is to save dogs and get them into their forever homes. *You can't just gather up all the sick dogs and keep them.* I went back and forth about what was the right thing to do. Finally, I've decided to keep her after all.

McMuffin is the very symbol of everything we want to do here. Her incredible health battles, her fighting spirit, her heroic comebacks, her kindness to others. She brings the best out of everybody else.

If ever she needs to go back and spend time at the vet's, like she did recently for an infection, the place just isn't the same without her. For two days, me and the nine other dogs, the whole sanctuary, felt there was a void, like something wasn't right. The McMuffin factor was just missing – and that's what she brings.

I love my life with the dogs, but sometimes I do get burned out. When this happens I always know what to do now. I just spend ten minutes with McMuffin, lying in a hammock together, and I'm ready to go again at full speed for the next two days. She's the most wonderful dog that was ever born.

When I think back to that broken dog hours from death and smelling of rotten flesh, I just can't comprehend it's the same dog. Her comeback and transition to where she is now is astonishing. If she can do it, so can you.

THIRTEEN

HOPE

It's one morning in October when my phone lights up with a call from Valeria. She's a young Ukrainian woman living out here, and like me, she feeds the dogs and is passionate about animal welfare.

Having undergone veterinary training herself, Valeria has seen all sorts of injuries, illnesses and infections in animals over the years. I'd describe her as generally unflappable. We're often exchanging WhatsApp messages, practical advice to do with dogs, stuff like that.

So when Valeria calls me, instead of our normal messaging, I know it's something serious. In fact, she's in a frantic state.

'Niall, we need you here immediately!' I can hear the panic in her voice, she's pretty much shouting.

'This dog is going to die, please come now Niall. Get here as fast as you can.'

I'd never heard Valeria like this before, so I grab my keys and jump on the scooter to find out what's going on. When I reach her ten minutes later, she's with another German lady, and both women are trying to soothe a very unhappy female dog. Catching sight of the three-inch nail rammed firmly into her left front leg, I can clearly see why the dog's whimpering.

On closer inspection, I realised I recognised this dog. I'd been feeding her for several months. Brown and black, medium sized and of no discernible mix of breeds, she was unremarkable to look at in every way. One of a bunch of twenty dogs dwelling in a little clearing, between some shacks where the migrant workers lived.

The dogs here in the jungle tend to gravitate towards where humans live because they know there'll be scraps of food lying around, a clean source of water and maybe, if they're lucky, some love and attention too.

The migrant work is seasonal though, so there's not people here all the time. We'd been making this little clearing a regular stop on the morning feeding rounds, in case the dogs weren't getting any food once the workers had moved on.

The dogs would all come from different areas, but I remembered this one girl would always hang around on the outskirts of the pack. Never pushing herself forward. She was shy, quiet, reserved. She brought no drama to anyone. She knew her place and was grateful for anything. There are millions of dogs like her.

I'd only really started paying her particular attention a few weeks back when she'd given birth to some puppies. I actually rescued one of her little ones – who I called

Pipsqueak because she was a tiny little mite who was so frightened that she refused to eat. Someone suggested she must associate food with something that had scared her, which seemed as good an explanation as any other. Far smaller than her siblings, she obviously wasn't big enough to make it in the jungle. I managed to whip Pipsqueak out to safety, and was overjoyed to find her a loving home in Bangkok. Pipsqueak got lucky, because only half of the other pups had survived. That's standard out here to be honest, though I don't write too much about it on my Insta, as people don't necessarily want the sad news.

After the puppies, we had got mummy dog successfully spayed, so she wouldn't have to go through it again, and I was pleased to see that she'd kept coming back for food ever since. So she was doing just fine – until now when she somehow had had this sharp metal instrument impaled into her fur.

There wasn't time for the three of us, Valeria, me and the German lady, to consider how the hell this nasty nail had managed to lodge itself so deeply into the leg. The important thing was getting it out of her. And quickly.

I fetched some pliers from a local fellow volunteer, and while they secured the poor, terrified mutt as she lay on the ground, I set about trying to extract the nail. Now I'm a 72 kg guy, and let me tell you it took every ounce of strength I could muster to get that bastard nail out of her. It took four almighty tugs until finally it came free.

'Good girl,' we all cooed, stroking her gently. 'You're a brave little soldier, aren't you.'

She wasn't a dog who naturally enjoyed human attention; we knew that she was on the shy side of dog personalities. But she was a tough cookie for sure. She hadn't tried to run from us at all while that nail had been embedded in her body. It was like she knew she was in big trouble, and she needed to let us help her.

Luckily, using her vet skills, Valeria was able to get the dog patched up, injected with antibiotics to ward off infection, and administer the urgent medical care needed. The one saving grace in this grisly situation was that it was a clean injury, and the dog's bone hadn't shattered.

She seemed in shock, unsurprisingly, but she would be OK. The kennels were still getting up to speed and were not quite ready for receiving dogs, but I managed to rearrange a few things and found a temporary solution because the case was so serious.

We all agreed it was a horrible injury and speculated about how it had happened. It's not like we have CCTV on all the street corners like there is in the UK. It's impossible to know really how and why things happen for the dogs, so there's guesswork and detective skills needed.

That night, I spoke to some local builders who confirmed that the nail could only have been fired from a nail gun, as you'd never have been able to pin her down and embed it so cleanly or deeply otherwise. Why the hell would anyone want to do that? She wasn't aggressive, she wasn't a nuisance. She was a totally nondescript dog, getting quietly on with her life.

Some dogs really stand out from the pack the first time you meet them, whether it's their striking looks or stand-out personalities. But not this one: she wasn't a leader, she wasn't a 'star'.

We wondered whether an accident might have happened somehow and she was in the wrong place at the wrong time. Yet she kept coming for food and we were able to keep a close eye on her, and we didn't think much more of it. There are always dogs to be worried about.

But a few weeks later, when I went on my usual feeding rounds, I spotted her and I saw something very worrying – there was a clear knife slash down the side of her neck. It looked like it had been made by a machete. And there was no way on earth it hadn't been done on purpose.

My heart sank. I realised the nail-gun incident was no accident either. This poor dog was being targeted and being deliberately abused by somebody. It seems completely unfathomable to most of us, that a human would want to inflict harm on any defenceless dog. Why?

If a dog is being a nuisance, it's not unheard of for humans to kill them. It doesn't bear thinking about, I know. But it happens. Dogs' throats can be slashed, or they can be poisoned. This seemed different. You wouldn't shoot a nail gun into the leg or slash a knife down the side of the neck unless you were purposely trying to inflict pain and abuse. This was some sicko enjoying torturing her.

Even if you could track down the person or people who had done this to her, it's impossible to try and bring any legal punishment for animal cruelty cases out here. There's just not the legislation for it sadly, as much as I would have liked someone to be held responsible for this hideous crime.

The knife wound, though nasty and relatively deep, was thankfully not life threatening. The big problem was trying to catch her, so we could treat it properly. Unfortunately, but not surprisingly, after the knife attack, the dog's behaviour had changed completely. She didn't want any of us remotely near her. Her trusting instinct had obviously been smashed to smithereens by whoever was inflicting this sick abuse.

I took the sedative pills to her area hoping that might allow her to be caught. We use sedatives when we need to catch wild dogs to be neutered or medically taken care of, but they aren't necessarily easy to administer. If you put the pills in a bowl of food, you can't guarantee the right dog will eat it. And if a dog will allow you to put the medicine directly in their mouth, then they're not the kind of animals who generally need to be sedated to be caught anyway.

But anything was worth a try. A gang of us, all seriously worried about her welfare, went up to the clearing area where she lived. We took jeeps and different dog-catching nets and leads, but all to no avail. She was just impossible to catch.

She recognised me too, so as soon as she spotted my face she'd scarper and know we were trying to get her. You could hardly blame her for being so wary. The other volunteers all persevered. We knew how important it was to help her.

Eventually, after ten days of efforts to get her, four of the other volunteers working together successfully managed to catch her. We were able to fix up the nasty knife wound without too many complications, but we knew there was no way we could put her back in her own habitat this time, and risk her suffering more violence and cruelty. She was too vulnerable. We needed to make her safe.

By this time the sanctuary was up and running, and we had somewhere to take her. So this poor victim of human abuse became one of the sanctuary's first residents. We had no idea what future lay in store for her, all we could do was hope. And that was the name we chose for her.

We certainly needed a lot of optimism with Hope, because she was in a very sorry state. Although her physical wounds could be fixed, the mental scars, like so many victims of abuse, would take far longer to heal.

Hope was a dog who was completely mentally shut down from the repeated abuse she'd suffered. She was broken. Her spirit was destroyed. She was unable to function as a normal dog.

She spent hours curled up in a ball, making her body as small as possible, and couldn't even muster the energy to walk. She always wanted complete privacy to go to the toilet (fair enough) but I'd have to carry her over to the bushes to do her business. It felt like lifting a 20 to 30-kg rock each time.

She didn't even have the basic instinct or desire to eat anymore. She must have been hungry. Yet her appetite for food, like life in general, had been run into the ground.

She was never remotely aggressive, which you might expect from a dog in her situation. Instead, she simply shut down, and didn't want to know about the world.

I recognised from my own depressive episodes how that felt. It was like she just didn't have the will to leave her own bed. And certainly there were times when I have been the same. I also recognised all the signs of post-traumatic abuse that I'd so painfully witnessed in my own mum all those years ago at the hands of her violent partner Andreas. Hope, who was likely only three years old, seemed to have given up on life. It was as if she had absolutely no hope at all.

I went to bed feeling a bit glum; I held Snoop a little closer to me that night, trying to use his warm furry mass as an anchor, to blot out some unhappy memories from my past which had been stirred up.

A day's work here, as much as I wouldn't want to be doing anything else, can leave me a little broken. The anxiety and depression are still part of who I am. Sadly, they never disappear forever. You just learn the tools to manage them and learn that after the darkness there will be light to follow.

Not for the first time since I set out on this mission, it was the kindness of strangers who lifted me up. After a bad run of luck at the weekend thinking about poor Hope, and running around trying to catch dogs to sterilise, I managed to break my flip-flops and wreck my running shoes. I ended up being so busy I was walking around with two right-foot flip-flops on. I shared my predicament on social media thinking it would make people laugh at the ridiculous state I was in. But the reaction wasn't just to chuckle, I had at least forty people asking me for my address to send me new shoes! A woman in America even sent me a picture of flip-flops to choose from in the shopping aisle and was heading to the post office next to airmail them to me. Bless her. I was blown away by that kindness.

I've learned now, after all these months, that if ever there is a moment where I am tired or soaking wet and doubt the mission, even for a second, I just need to think about the people supporting me and spurring me on. They have never met me in person, and yet I feel across the oceans that they know me and are my friends and are passionate about helping animals too. Reading those lovely messages makes a difference and picks me up when I'm low. They really keep me going and touch my heart.

For me the most exciting thing is the number of parents who contact me saying their kids watch the dogs' progress when they are having breakfast every morning. I have to pinch myself at that thought because that could possibly be shaping a young mind for their entire life to be kind to dogs. The young and their natural love for animals is crucial in the work I do. I've started giving talks to kids, and have set up YouTube videos about the work we do, because if we can inspire the children they will help educate the adults in their lives.

It's fundamentally the brave, resilient dogs and kind, big-hearted people that get me over and through all the inevitable challenges.

I know how everyone across the world is so strapped for cash right now, the cost of living crisis is affecting us all, so I never fail to take for granted any donations, which always go 100 per cent towards the dogs' health and their life-saving treatments. These donations literally make saving dogs' lives possible.

And the messages of support I receive lift my spirits when they flag and confirm that this crucial work must carry on. It's as if, when I head off up the mountain laden with dog food, I honestly feel there are wonderful people willing me on, and it means the absolute world to me.

Hope's recovery was slow. The name hope seemed so ironic, as here was a dog who just didn't seem to have any. It had been sucked out of her. But we still prayed that eventually she would turn a corner. That a good life, the one she really deserved, would be waiting for her one day.

She started walking herself to go to the loo, rather than letting me carry her. Only at a snail's pace, but it was progress. It took one metre at a time to coax her to walk, and she would be rewarded with food. Other times it was clear she didn't want company and just needed to decompress a little by herself.

Her fur had now grown back, and you couldn't even see the scars from the knife and the nail gun's damage. But the mental scars ran deep. I still wasn't confident she would ever be able to live normally, and I worried about her, but I refused to give up on her.

And the patience started paying off. After four weeks, Hope was coming out for walks with the others and taking herself off into the hedges to go to the loo. She'd always run straight back into her kennel afterwards mind you, but I thought it was sweet that she found comfort there, with her cosy blankets and bedding. It was the first time in her life she'd had anything that was her own. It was her safe place. We all need those.

We gradually got her eating more enthusiastically, and coming for proper walks with the others. Her tail lifted higher, as did her head. It was like she was at long last believing there might be a place for her on this little planet after all. I was so relieved.

After five to six weeks, the ever wonderful McMuffin had succeeded in making Hope feel secure enough to play a little bit. McMuffin by now was acting like a therapy dog, she was such a natural carer. King Whacker (not long now till you meet him) was also a gentleman with her. It was really genuinely touching how the others rallied round and it shows what a difference a few good friends can make.

A truly joyful day came when Hope rolled over and showed me her belly, meaning 'go on then, you can now give me a rub please, Niall'. It was a sign she trusted me, and wanted me to touch her, and that was a huge honour.

I'm in no way an animal psychologist or expert on behaviour or anything like that, but you learn by patiently watching dogs how they might be feeling. You have to try and figure it out from their point of view. Hope, because of her awful previous experiences with humans, was very much thinking 'these people will hurt you'. We needed to show her we wouldn't.

It took three months of living in the sanctuary for her to start leading anything that resembled a normal dog life and start letting her guard down. She's firmly one of the pack now. These days, Hope is a completely different dog from the abuse victim we first met. For 80 per cent of the time at least, she lets her guard down. I can sense there is still a small part of her thinking, 'this is too good to be true, it won't stay like this forever,' but generally there is a lightness about her now that I wasn't sure would ever be possible for Hope.

She goes on runs and she's really got her personality back. She's actually a very loving dog, and especially good with the puppies. You can totally see that she's been a mum before, she's done it and knows what she's doing. That maternal instinct is in her.

What I love about Hope is that she's living proof for victims of abuse that life won't always be dark. There is light on the other side.

If you met her in the future without knowing her backstory, you'd probably think she was withdrawn or maybe even boring for a dog. She might not look at you directly or want affection. Even though everything would look perfect on the outside, you could judge her and cast her off as not a great fun dog.

I think the same is true of people. We all carry hidden scars (not necessarily physical) and are experts at hiding them. It could be addiction, being unfaithful to a partner, depression, not being able to have a baby, anxiety, grief, regret, abuse, financial ruin or any number of other bad things out there.

* * *

And now the best thing that I dream for every dog has happened for Hope.

A few months ago, a girl called Steff from England wanted to come and visit the sanctuary and help out looking after the dogs and walking and feeding them. I get lots of people asking me if they can do this, and it's my dream one day to be able to say yes to more and have an organised programme for volunteers. But currently that's not quite possible. However, I did agree to Steff coming.

We took the dogs for a special day out at the beach. Just like humans, I firmly believe they deserve some treats in their lives. On the way home driving I saw in the back mirror Steff give Hope a little kiss on the head and whisper in her ear, which wouldn't be unusual for a dog lover, and I smiled. It was amazing to see Hope accept the affection like this, and look back at Steff with real warmth and trust in her eyes, especially considering the uphill battles we'd had with her.

Three days later, Steff messaged me on WhatsApp. 'I would love to take Hope back to England with me,' she wrote. 'Would you mind terribly if I was able to do that for her?'

Would I mind? I was bloody overjoyed! Steff said she was really nervous to ask because she thought that I had such an attachment to Hope, and vice versa, but she said that she and Hope had really bonded. Hope had come so far in life and now Steff really wanted to give her a forever home, safe and sound in England.

Steff is now preparing the paperwork for Hope to travel back to England with her where she'll live with Steff's loving family. She'll need a winter coat, and some warmer clothes, but this is the perfect happy-ever-after for Hope, who I was never sure would come out of her shell.

It felt so significant and healing for me from a personal perspective too. I might not have been able to protect my mum from getting beaten up and abused in my youth. But I *had* been able to offer a safe refuge for Hope.

I don't claim to be a great life coach, but I hope that there might be people reading about Hope, and all her battles, and be able to take some comfort from the fact that life *can* change. You may feel like a defenceless victim, but you are stronger inside than you might think.

Please don't give up on yourselves. Like Hope, and like my mum, there will be lightness after the dark times. There can be escapes from the pain. And with time, love and patience you too can have a bright and positive future.

Hope might just be a dog that is likely thousands of miles away from where you are. But Hope is so much more. She could be any one of us or any friend. She shows that with a little love, some friends and the basics, anything is possible.

FOURTEEN

THE ONE
WHO ESCAPED
MURDER

Day to day here in Koh Samui can feel like a mixture between being in a hospital triage centre and out on a battlefield with an army. That might sound like a complete over-exaggeration but it is very much the case for the street and jungle dogs.

Broken limbs, puppies being born daily, dogs with open wounds, severe illness, dogs being dumped, dogs being attacked by humans, massive fights, and so on. You never know what you are going to walk into.

I got a frantic series of calls one lunchtime about a dog from a Russian lady on the other side of the island. That's far from unusual, lots of people have somehow got my number here and can sometimes treat it like it's the fourth emergency service. If there's a dog that needs help, it's 'pick up the phone to Niall'. Tourists call and they're understandably worried, but lots of the time it's not quite a drop-everything-and-dash-to-the-scene emergency they believe. I can get around twenty calls like this in a day. I just can't physically respond to every single one.

However, as soon as I saw the picture pop up on my phone from the Russian lady, I knew I needed to get there urgently. She wasn't freaking out over nothing. I'd never seen anything like it. The photo clearly showed this poor dog had purposely been attacked by a human, hell bent on killing the old boy by physically splitting his head open. It was one of the most shocking things I'd ever seen.

I grabbed my scooter – my jeep was out of action and fixing it up was on my to-do list – and must have broken every speed limit known to man racing across to the other side of the island in twenty-five minutes. My knuckles were white from gripping the handlebar so hard, my jaw was tensely set and my adrenaline pumping madly by the time I arrived at the scene.

There was an atmosphere of hysteria outside the lady's house. Someone had sensibly corralled the poor terrified dog into a cordoned-off area in the front yard, away from the family's kids. This was certainly not a sight for young eyes. I felt fairly squeamish myself if I'm honest, as well as rising panic about what action to take.

I've started to keep some basic medicines at home, stuff like antibiotics, painkillers and tick and flea treatments. But I knew there was nothing I had on the bike or at home that would be able to help this time.

I crouched down to have a better look. 'Hey buddy, what's happened to you eh?' His eyes were wide and plead-ing. He knew he was in a right mess. The gash was deep and right down the centre of his forehead. Despite the blood, which had clotted around the fur, you could literally see into the poor animal's brain and other parts of his anatomy.

Dogs who've been injured and are in pain can act unpredictably, they can snarl and bite. I mean, wouldn't you? It's hardly surprising if they've experienced some horrific trauma like this, inflicted by human hands.

I needed to take this incredibly gently. Very slowly, I reached out to touch him and gave his belly a careful rub to distract him enough to be able to edge a little closer towards the nasty head wound. 'We're going to try and fix you up buddy,' I soothed, peering cautiously and worried by the depth and width of the gash.

He must have been in a whole world of pain, as for twenty minutes I talked to him, while on the phone trying to get hold of some form of transport. Yet he was weirdly calm.

It was almost unnerving. He should, quite understandably, have been going ballistic at me. Yet he sensed I was here to help, not cause more harm.

He was in such a delicate state, seemingly hanging onto life by a thread, so I knew there was no way I could get him on the scooter. The wound was so precisely between his eyes that it was not possible this was an accident. Someone must have done this on purpose. It absolutely beggars belief a human could try and finish a dog off in this way.

I gently put my hand on his belly and could feel the rise and fall of his frightened breathing. Stroking his soft fur to soothe him, I managed to sort out a truck to come for us. I had no idea whether any dog could survive this; the injury seemed so severe that in my heart I felt it was unlikely, but I knew I had to try and get him to the vet.

Some kindly locals fetched some towels and I carefully, carefully scooped him up into the back of the truck and climbed up beside him.

He was so calm and trusting. I felt acutely conscious that the slightest move in the wrong direction might hit a nerve, sever an artery and kill him. That ten-minute drive to the vet's surgery felt like a lifetime. I cradled his body in my lap, comforting him the whole time with what I'd describe as some kind of doggy 'sweet nothings' in his ear. 'We're going to try and help you, fella,' I soothed. 'Just hang in there for me, good boy.'

He was obviously a little distressed, and each bump in the road brought a little whimper from him and a wince from me in sympathy, but he remained incredibly calm considering his brain was almost hanging out. I wondered whether he was in severe shock as other dogs in that situation would have been.

I'd rung ahead to warn the vet I was bringing in an emergency case, and as soon as we arrived at the surgery everyone cleared the way for us and he was rushed straight into theatre. I stood at the reception desk as he was taken in, wondering if he'd come out alive. It seemed a lot to hope for.

'Fill in the patient's name please,' said the receptionist, passing me the white sheet of paper that was now familiar to me, and an old biro. That is always the first question they ask at the vet's of course, and one I really hadn't had time to think about. My own brain felt about as fried and fucked up as the poor dog's was at this stage.

So I just wrote down 'whack' as he'd had a big whack to his head. But that looked weird, I couldn't just call him whack. Hastily I added an 'er' at the end. And 'Whacker' became his name.

He was quickly put under anaesthetic while the vet made a proper inspection. He wasn't sure if the dog could be saved. But he'd give it his best shot.

The staff at the vet's all knew me by now, and we speculated in the waiting room about what could have happened to Whacker. It seemed like our boy had been attacked by something like a pickaxe or a garden trowel, with the definite intention of killing him in one firm blow to the head. The locals told me that five dogs the previous year had been poisoned in the same area where Whacker had been found. Perhaps whoever was doing it thought this method would be quicker than poisoning?

Indeed, half a millimetre either way would have resulted in the dog's immediate death.

His survival, the vet said, would all depend on the next twelve hours. The vet seemed to think if he pulled through that critical window, he might be OK.

There was nothing else I could do but head home and wait. I knew Whacker was in safe hands, but I didn't get much sleep as my mind was too busy worrying about him or thinking about the horrible brutality he'd suffered. It wasn't the first case of animal abuse I'd come across, but it was certainly the most graphic I'd yet to witness. How could anyone do that to an innocent animal?

The next day I was straight round to the vet's. Whacker had survived the night! The relief was palpable. He'd been stitched up and he was to be kept in and monitored for the day. The poor thing looked like a right old scary mess though. The vet had to put a special pipe into the wound to drain away all the blood, pus and fluid (for want of a more medical term, I called this 'brain juice' – you probably get my drift).

He was clearly in pain, and as well as the poorly head, Whacker had all the other problems common to street dogs, with fleas and ticks and general malnourishment, but these things can all be sorted out and fixed with some TLC.

Whacker had to be kept clean to avoid infection, and so the vet had put a large plastic cone on his head for protection, to stop him banging or scratching or getting the wound dirty. If you've ever taken a pet for any small surgery, you'll know what these are. And generally the animals get very annoyed by them and want them off as soon as possible.

This dog however, who the vet guessed was between six and eight years old, wouldn't fight the cone at all. Perhaps the dogs back home are a bit more diva-like, or perhaps the dogs here are just so grateful for any medical care they accept it better. Who knows, but he was such a gentle softie.

In fact, he didn't just accept the cone, he genuinely seemed proud of it, as if to say 'Look at me! I'm getting all fixed up here!'

I took him to the sanctuary where we could care for him in the immediate aftermath of the surgery, and he would prance around in the cone holding his head up high, almost like it was a status symbol. A strutting sign to show off the fact he was being cared for, looked after and taken good care of now. You got this, Whacker!

The pride with which he wore the cone gave him quite a regal air, it made him look like a little king, trotting around, and so King Whacker he then became.

He'd be back and forth to the vet's a lot during those two to three weeks of recovery, and I dared to hope that the brave little fella really would make it after all, as he came on little walks with me, just in the grounds initially, seeming to improve a bit more every single day.

He's such a lovely friendly dog, and so eager to meet people, I decided that the most likely scenario for his attack was that he was always hanging around the wrong place. If he'd made himself a frequent visitor at someone's home, or a fancy resort, or a smart private area, his presence might not have been at all wanted. He also liked to dig holes in the earth, and if you're trying to make your place look appealing, you want to get rid of that problem. You want to get rid of the dog.

I concluded that being the big, innocent, goofy, all-round nice guy that King Whacker was, probably turned out to be the very thing that was nearly his undoing.

It brought me such joy to see his progress. There's always a leader in every pack of dogs, they need one and rely on one, and King Whacker is a leader like no other. While other alpha dogs throw their weight around to assert their authority in standard ways, like snarling, or fighting, or hoarding food to show the beta members who's in charge, King Whacker doesn't do any of this. He doesn't need to, he's simply the boss, the king, and they all respect that. He happily prances around controlling the pack with never any need to show off his muscles or aggression.

Like a true king, they all look up to him, and he leads by example. He's the first to go into his kennel nice and orderly. He waits patiently for his food. If another dog is acting out, Whacker controls them with one stern look or little prod of his snout. He's one of the larger dogs, but he's in no way massive, or ever uses his size against anyone else.

He's like you would imagine the perfect dad, who's come in from work after a long day at the office and yet still finds the energy and patience to roll around on the floor playing with his kids.

Adorably, all the younger puppies race each other, full of beans and life, and King Whacker plays a game where he pretends that he can't catch up with them, even though of course he really could, because he's bigger, faster and stronger. He's nothing to prove.

The top dog really sets the tone for the rest of the pack, and King Whacker behaves impeccably and they all just follow suit.

He is truly an honourable, wonderful creature who has taught me that miracles do happen and you need to grab every moment of joy you can. From the very moment he arrived in my life, with his gaping wound, and then being all stitched up, he's quite simply never skipped a beat in terms of enjoying his life.

Going on his runs. Digging his holes in the sand. He loves every second, living it to the full as though it might be his last.

More than anyone, King Whacker has taught me that whatever hiccups you've had in your life – and having your head split open is an almighty big one – you shouldn't let it stop your fun.

He has no grievances with anybody, he only has love to share. He bounced back with positivity. Inspired by him, I vowed not to get worked up about the violence he'd so cruelly suffered, but instead work to educate people better.

The plan was always to find King Whacker somewhere safe back on the streets once he had healed. However, several people expressed interest in giving him a forever home. More than a few in fact; this glorious animal was so popular from sharing posts of him on social media, there were over fifty people, from all over the world, applying to offer him a home. There are a few details to work out, but King Whacker will lead the life he now deserves and will travel to his forever home in the coming summer.

Someone tried to kill him but yet again an incredible dog proves that miracles *do* happen, and this time good triumphed over bad.

FIFTEEN

ONCE BEYOND SAVING ... BUT NOW GOING STRONG

If there were more humans in the world like Derek, then I swear the world would be a better place. He's gentle, he's unassuming and he's full of gratitude for the little he has. I've learned so much from spending time with this humble street dog, he's something of a hero to me now. The most selfless soul you could ever meet.

Born and bred on the streets of Koh Samui, and of no identifiable breed, he'd never had anything to call his own, he'd never had any human to show him affection, and every single meal in his life had been hard won and scavenged for. Life, like for so many of these dogs, had been challenge after challenge.

He wasn't on anyone's radar really until Rod scooped him up and told me there was a dog, which he'd already named Derek, in dire need. The sanctuary on the land that I'd long been dreaming about was finally ready to receive its first set of residents. Could I, Rod asked, take this one in?

I hadn't seen pictures of this dog or any video footage, but I trusted Rod completely. And if he judged that a dog needed help, then I knew that's what I would try and provide.

I have to admit though, it was a proper shock after Rod dropped him off and I first caught sight of him. He was a decent age, probably 10, maybe even 12. There was very little of his fur left, and in the colder wet month of that October, he was shivering with no natural barrier to the elements, letting out spontaneous whimpers.

His skin was in the worst state I've ever seen for a dog – with the exception of McMuffin and her tumours. There were infected wounds with blood, pus and some awful black gunk oozing out of them too.

Christ almighty.

Every inch of his poor pathetic body was just repugnant. There really was no other way to describe it.

We took him to the vet, who took his bloods. His results were too dismal for much to be done. 'This dog should rightly be dead with these results,' the vet warned me. 'He's past saving, I'm afraid.'

However, I'd had this pessimism before with vets, like in the case of McMuffin. I felt it was worth giving the old boy a little bit more of a chance, so I took his blood test results to a second vet.

'This dog is virtually dead, he's finished,' confirmed the second vet, who said he might not even last another hour. 'There really isn't much we can do.'

The poor creature had a lethal combination of blood parasites, skin disease, mange and about a thousand – I'm not exaggerating – tiny fleas and little fruit flies crawling all over his skin and going into the wounds. His red blood cells, white blood cells and platelets were all so chronically low because of his anaemia, it didn't seem reversible.

The vet said that even trying to treat him with the basic medicines to kill the fleas would probably kill him as his body was too weak to take it.

It wasn't what I wanted to hear of course, but I had to accept the fact that not all dogs could be saved. Some of them were just beyond it. So I took him back to the sanctuary. The least I could do was make sure his life's end was comfortable. I removed as many fleas as possible but he was sore to the touch.

Because we had only just finished building the kennels on the land, they were still incredibly basic. The cement was freshly dried but cold. The poor old boy had barely any fur left to keep him warm and we hadn't furnished the kennels with any proper beds at that stage.

All I could think of was to go home and get the duvet from my own bed and put it there for him to curl up on for the night. And I couldn't even touch him properly, he was sore and flinched when I had a go at removing some of the fleas. But I wanted to show him I was there for him, so I used my little finger on the tiny parts of fur still present. 'I'm for you, buddy,' I whispered, caressing his little paw.

Maybe it's not a bad thing that he will be out of his misery soon, I wondered.

I felt so sad for him. At least he had a roof over his head and a duvet to snuggle in. I could manage at the end of his life to try and offer him as much dignity and comfort as I could.

I said goodnight to him, and shut the door, feeling certain he would be dead come the morning. I felt sorry that I'd never get to know him and wondered where I would need to dig his burial patch the next day.

I slept fitfully that night, and by 6 am I was wide awake and ready to face whatever state I was going to find him in. It was still dark at that time when I drove to the sanctuary. On arrival and bracing myself, I opened the door to his kennel … and was stunned to find he was still breathing. Somehow, he'd survived the night. And then he made it through another one, and then another one. I spent four days convinced I would find him dead the next time, but he was just hanging in there, against all expectations. After four nights I decided Derek was very much like Del Boy Trotter, the likeable chancer from *Only Fools and Horses*, who, however many lows he hits, picks himself right back up. A natural born survivor.

All Derek did was sleep, and he drank a lot of water, as if he couldn't quench a thirst. After five days of seeming to exist at death's door, I felt like perhaps he was stronger than we'd all given him credit for. Gingerly, because I was wary of all his sores, I applied some of the flea powder, and after a week caring for him, we'd got rid of all the little bugs crawling on the wounds which made me feel happy. Maybe Derek had a few more weeks in him after all? I was happy that his last few days were more comfortable.

But against all the odds and expert predictions, Derek just kept hanging on and hanging on in there. His blood tests showed a little progress, maybe the cell counts were a little higher, and we were able to start feeding him medicine to ward off the bugs. Slowly, there was a slight improvement. The medicine was starting to work.

After two weeks his eyes looked, not exactly alive and certainly not shining, but let's just say they looked a little bit less dead than they were before. His appetite was returning and he was still drinking a lot of water, so I felt he wasn't ready to give in yet. It seemed Derek wanted to live. He'd make it out of the critical stage.

After a month he went from barely being able to lift his head off the pillow to actually venturing outside the kennel to do his own toileting. He was always keen to head straight back to his kennel, mind you. But to everyone's astonishment, Derek was still going strong three months after he had been taken in.

I shared some pictures of his progress online and people soon became obsessed with him. It was like he'd risen from the dead somehow. It really captured people's imagination; they took this sorry creature with his puppy-dog sad eyes into their hearts.

One day I took him on a little walk, only for 100 metres or so, but it felt like a major achievement. I was over the moon. What's more, Derek actually started trying to speak to me. Yes, I know how daft that sounds, but honest to God he makes these little growl noises, more like a little sing-song, that is his dog-speak. It might sound like 'Rrrreeefaw' to those of you not fluent in the language of dogs. But I can hear it perfectly clearly. 'Look at me, Niall. I'm still here, eh? There's life in the old dog after all,' he seems to say. Followed by, 'Now give me some more food please.' If you were here with Derek, I know you would understand his language too.

The most endearing thing about Derek is how proud and attached he is to his little kennel, or his 'VIP suite' as I like to call it. As a street dog he'd had to scavenge for everything, from food to water, and had never been treated to the miracles of medicine before. Suddenly, he'd been given his own freshly painted little house with a proper bed. It was all his!

People who had followed his miraculous recovery sent blankets and soft toys for him and he was loving it all. It might have looked like a humble kennel to anyone else, but as far as Derek was concerned, he'd landed on his paws and bagged himself the Taj Mahal – with room service twice a day.

Derek really taught me that possessions and fancy stuff don't mean anything. All it takes to make him happy and exuberant and fulfilled is just this tiny little space with a roof over his head, food he doesn't have to fight or scavenge for, and a tiny bit of love.

His fur is coming back. It just gets better by the day, the strands are pushing through the skin and are a lovely golden sort of auburn colour mixed in with black and a few greys, fitting for his age. He sometimes shivers a little and feels the cold but he has snuggly pyjamas for cooler or wetter nights, and still enjoys a belly rub where the holes are. His lovely dopey eyes are warm and happy and melt all our hearts.

He doesn't exude pus these days, or ugly black gunk; the only thing dripping out of him is his angelic, beautifully understated charisma.

He's a little gentle soul who doesn't want to bark at anybody, scuffle with anybody, and loves to hand me his paw.

Of course Derek is old now, and he will die at some stage, but he will die in the happiest retirement home. He's the one dog that will never get adopted. I couldn't possibly expect him to leave the little place he is so proud to call home. He'll end his days here, being well loved and looked after.

Derek is living proof to me that no matter how bad things are, or how down you feel, try never to give up. The situation might seem catastrophic one minute, but a couple of months later you could be running along the beach without a care in the world. He appreciates every second of his life, and I try to live by that example.

While on the subject of miraculous recoveries, remember that little pup Rodney who we met at the very start of the book? Red raw and basically a ball of scabby, scaly, pus-y mank?

Not a patch of skin on him was unaffected. I stayed up with him all night in my office with him wrapped in blankets, and it was fifty–fifty whether he'd make it through that first night.

Well, I am absolutely over the moon to report that with some basic medicine and a lot of TLC, that pup just went from strength to strength. Fed up on fatty steak and fresh mackerel, the little fella eventually made a full and complete recovery. This is just the dream for me.

I am mentioning him now, with Derek's story, because they shared very similar, horribly dramatic skin conditions. Like Derek before him, little Rodders also had a huge turnabout in his health. In fact, that pathetic little melon-sized pup enjoyed one of the best comebacks I've seen of all time.

Derek and Rodders became best buds, with the older Derek taking the pup under his wing. They're devoted to one another. It's very special when you see animals form these bonds.

I shared Rodney's story online and – oh my God! – did people fall head over heels with that tiny soul! The Del Boy and Rodney comedy act charmed us all, even those people who'd never heard of *Only Fools and Horses*.

Whereas Derek's recovery was relatively slow, being an older dog, Rodney's happened in a matter of weeks. It was like every day as he grew and all his cells renewed, he just got better and better. I could tell from almost the start he would become a big boy one day, as his paws were always vastly out of proportion with the rest of him. And day by day his skin cleared up and healed beautifully and his lovely grey fur started coming back.

He's now 100 per cent recovered, unrecognisable from that horrific state Rod found him in. He's glowing with good health and energy and has a cheeky personality – and a fondness for ice cream these days. Best of all, when I asked the army of dog fans who follow me on Instagram if anyone could offer little Rodders a forever home, over 200 people applied. Can you believe it?

It absolutely makes my heart sing that there are so many people putting themselves forward now to adopt dogs and pups. I've got a good system up and running, where wannabe dog owners fill in a form and we screen them and have video calls and all the normal things you would do to check they are genuine animal lovers and would be a suitable match for the dogs' needs and personalities. It will make such a difference to these animals' future, having an owner who will love them and cherish them as they deserve to be.

Little Rodney will go to his new forever home thanks to a lovely couple who can't wait to make him part of their lives. They live in Wales, so I'll be sending Rodney off with a raincoat, but I know how rosy his future will now be. Will I miss him? Of course I will. As will Derek. That little guy has brought such joy to all of us here, as well as to people following his story online. He's one of the most popular dogs I've ever met. But finding him a real home is more important than me keeping him here.

This is what I want for all the dogs. They have to come first, and their welfare is everything.

In a sad postscript to this chapter, not all stories have a happy ending. Animal rescue is by nature tough, and there is plenty of bad news and challenges.

It was in October when I had a major, personal setback. Lucky, the very first dog I fell in love with in Koh Samui, had always been special to me. After months of being a loner, she'd happily hooked up with little Chopper, an infectiously cheerful little pup who'd been abandoned. They were inseparable, and it made my heart sing for joy when I could give them the treats they deserved in life, like taking them for days at the beach. Nobody has it tougher than the dogs, so a little fun along the way at the weekends is what we all need.

Then one autumn day, the pair simply vanished and have never been seen since.

I loved them both dearly, especially given that Lucky came first and was the whole reason for beginning the mission to help dogs.

It goes without saying I exhausted every option in terms of finding them, hunting high and low with many wonderful volunteers lending a hand. Everyone adored Lucky and Chopper and knew how close to my heart they'd become.

I will never know for sure what happened to them, or where they went. But for my own sanity I have to not get hung up on it. There are so many other dogs that need help. I'm 95 per cent sure – and have to hope – that Lucky and Chopper are safe and have just moved on with humans (a large number of people come and go in the area and Chopper did have an 'owner' at the start who gave him a collar). There is 3 per cent of me who believes they might be deeper in the jungle somewhere with migrant farmers and will come back one day. And there is also, I'm sad to say, a small 2 per cent of me which thinks something bad has happened to them, or someone took them after seeing them on social media.

Dogs do go missing, it's just part of life. But it's certainly the hardest part of doing this. Dealing with a sick or injured dog is one thing, I know where I am with that. But not knowing where they are is a killer. I just have to save more dogs and use them to drive me on to do so. If I sit around and mope or get angry that's not going to help save more dogs.

All I can do is to remain relentlessly positive. Some dogs reappear. This may seem dramatic, or silly to some people, but there honestly isn't an hour in the day when I don't think about Lucky and Chopper. I often just jump on my moped and go on an aimless drive looking for them. I live in hope that I will see that beautiful little pair again one day.

SIXTEEN

TIME FOR PROPER FOOD

For the first nine months when I started out helping stray dogs, my biggest concern was just getting empty bellies filled. The dogs were clearly starving, and buying kibble for them was the obvious and quickest answer. First from the local store, then buying in bulk at the wholesaler to make it more cost efficient. My head was so full of sterilising plans and how best to fund these, the nutrition and diet of the dogs took a back seat initially.

But by November, once we had the sanctuary established, I was ready to start thinking about making them proper meals. I realised feeding them all would be more efficient if I made the food fresh. It would be cheaper (saving more cash for the all-important sterilising), and it would be more healthy and nutritious, warding off later health issues (I hoped) and saving on costly vet bills down the line.

What's more, it would be tastier for the dogs. They gobbled up the kibble out of necessity, but it wasn't particularly enjoyable. Would you like to munch through a load of cardboard just to stop your tummy rumbling? Me neither.

I wanted to really get my head around the food situation, and offered to help some of the local dog-feeding volunteer groups.

I really do want to be clear throughout all this that I am not the first person to be helping street dogs in Thailand. I am no saviour treading where others have not dared to, or been bothered to, not in the slightest. I would hate anyone to think this is what I'm claiming just because I might have a louder voice and online presence.

Many other people here in Koh Samui have been doing all this – feeding and trying to neuter and care for animals – for far longer than I have. I absolutely take my hat off to all of them.

What I didn't realise before I got involved in the dog business was there is a real dog helping 'scene' here. There can be real rivalry between the various dog charities, organisations and volunteer groups, as there can in any other walk of life or workplace. There are so many volunteers and everybody's got their own way of doing things. It's a bit like baking: you've got your mum's wet cake recipe, but everybody thinks their own mum's way is better. At the end of the day, everybody's just trying their best, but still people will be judging the other methods too.

Everyone has their own ideas about what and how to feed. By spending time with the volunteers I saw how many of them were cooking rice and mixing it with the kibble to make it go further. They were also adding leftovers donated by restaurants, plus bones, stock or their own personal touches to make it tastier and to bulk it out.

They were all doing this individually and with real passion and love, but I realised it was labour intensive and doubled the time it takes to look after the dogs.

After coming from a business background, and knowing how crucial efficiency is if you want to make everything run smoothly and be successful, I found this a bit frustrating. I offered to batch cook all the food, then it would just be me getting up at the crack of dawn, not everyone, and then they could save that cooking time and use it to distribute the food instead. I felt it made sense. Though I was conscious that me coming in as a newcomer might ruffle feathers or put noses out of joint. Something I never intended to do.

One of my friends, an older German lady, has been feeding around 300 dogs for years, and I felt a bit embarrassed to tell the truth when my story attracted more of an interest online. Not that she was remotely bothered by that I'm sure, her focus is on the dogs, and doing her best by them, as is mine. But you can probably relate to how I felt.

What I could clearly see was that the dogs loved the home cooking much more than the dried food on its own. They devoured it in a totally joyous way, with gusto and enthusiasm, salivating as it was being served, tails wagging, big pink tongues lapping up every last morsel, which was wonderful to see. These dogs have so little pleasure or advantage in life that being able to make their eating experience enjoyable seemed the least we could offer. Especially as it was cheaper.

It made far more sense to start making fresh food, buying rice, vegetables and meat in bulk from the wholesalers and markets. I spoke to pet experts and nutritionists and the volunteers already working with the dogs, to learn all about what they'd eat, and between us we devised some basic recipes that wouldn't bankrupt us.

Rice is the cheapest thing to buy, and very filling, and I discovered that some coconut oil is good for them as well as being effective in binding it all together. Vegetables are great because you can use whatever is in season and the cheapest, like carrots, pumpkins and cabbage, all work nicely. Eggs, including even the shells, are excellent sources of protein. Fresh meat is always going to be more costly, but some of the brown chicken meat can go a long way. Also chicken blood is even better value, and makes it tastier for them. It might not appeal to you and me, but canines enjoy it, I promise!

I found a big wholesale supermarket and pretty much emptied them out of chicken blood in that first week. I went and sourced the biggest industrial-sized pots and pans I could find to make vast batches of meals, and enlisted the help and goodwill of as many volunteers as I could who would offer to lend a hand with distributing it.

Because of my chef background, I was used to making food on a large scale, so I didn't find the idea of cooking for several hundred dogs a week particularly daunting. I was thrilled to be able to put some skills from my earlier life to good use, and had a hunch that the 'customers' would be a damn sight more appreciative than some of the rich and famous I'd served before.

I rented out a local kitchen cheaply, which I made sure was central enough for volunteers to be able to come to each day to collect the homemade food, and was soon doing 200 kg of food per day. That allowed me to create about 5,000 meals a week. The satisfaction of being able to sort these practical matters out was immense.

We tried a range of recipes to discover ones the dogs would love, and though Snoop sleeps most of the day, I dragged him out of his retirement to put him to work. I gave him the job title of CTO – Chief Tasting Officer! You can never be too careful with quality control and good old Snoop takes his job very seriously.

I also started wondering that if we made the food really decent, perhaps pet owners might even buy it from us and then we could raise more cash for things like medicines and sterilising. Perhaps other volunteers in other parts of the country would be able to replicate the dishes and feed their street dogs well and cheaply, too? You know me by now, I'm always full of big plans …

There were logistical issues to iron out of course, storage concerns and other elements to work out, but I knew it was very do-able. We found old coconuts or palm leaves to serve the food on, dished up with large ladles from the pots. I smiled thinking of how I might describe some of the dishes on menus when I was a chef, like 'Duck risotto with braised pumpkin and Asian cabbage'.

'Here you go fellas,' I grinned, spooning it out for the happy campers. 'Bon appétit!'

A local Thai restaurant woman cooks the food. The recipe features rice, chicken stock, carrots, pumpkins, eggs, duck neck, cabbage and coconut oil. It's made to be as cheap and wholesome as possible for the dogs, and tasty too – if you closed your eyes and I gave you a spoonful I think you'd like it!

The best part is that it used to cost around $30 a day to feed the 80 dogs with a mixture of dry and tinned food. The new food costs around $90 a day which feeds 800.

The saving is insane, and means that the local volunteers who feed the dogs can use any spare cash they have on medicine rather than food. At some point I'd like to start adding supplements to improve their overall health.

Being able to improve the food situation so dramatically feels like real progress, and the online followers really love seeing the doggies lapping up their home-cooked meals.

I enjoy posting online about the dogs and what I'm up to, and it's effective because people want to help. I couldn't manage without the messages of support to lift my spirits on tough days. And the generosity of donations blows my mind, as well as providing crucial financial means to actually carry out the work. I guess by now I'm reasonably experienced at it.

But I've constantly got imposter syndrome, and when people write things on Instagram saying I'm 'an angel' or a 'hero' and stuff, I die of embarrassment and feel like a fraud to be honest. Angels and heroes are the people fighting fires and looking after the sick for a living: NHS workers, social workers, firefighters, teachers ... People who help starving children, people like that are the genuine heroes here. Not me.

I feel desperately uncomfortable by the thought of turning any of what I do into some kind of glory-gathering mission. But I wonder whether there are people who might accuse me of this, and it can make me anxious.

There's no right or wrong way to care for street dogs. It's a chronic problem out here that's very hard to fix and everybody's trying their best little way to do it. I couldn't do even a small part of this without all the help and support I get. I've had vets in other countries who offer advice on X-rays for free, pet shops who give me discounts, friends who help film the videos I share online. It constantly amazes me that all these people are willing to share their expertise with me and help out in so many ways.

★　★　★

It was December time and I was reflecting on the fact that I'd been feeding the dogs for almost a year. I'd also been sober for almost two years. Two hugely important achievements in my life which I never take for granted.

I was out doing the second feed of the day. I don't always do that, but if there are dogs who are in need of another meal I make sure to fit in another round in the evening.

I spotted my friend Rod coming over the hill, which was unusual at that time. He feeds the dogs too, but he wouldn't normally be in this area at this particular time. I always enjoy seeing Rod, yet I felt a twinge of anxiety at that moment, he was riding faster than usual and seemed on a mission to get to me.

And as soon as Rod drew close enough for me to see his anguished face, paler than normal and with a tightly clenched jaw, I knew something had happened.

'Hit me with it then, Rod,' I said, as soon as he'd dismounted his bike. There was no point beating around the bush. 'What's going on?'

'One of your guys has been hit,' he told me.

'Who is it?' I said, heart sinking. I thought about the direction Rod had emerged from, and deduced it would be someone in Bubba's pack, one of my original gang. I felt like I knew the answer before he responded.

'It's the old boy,' said Rod. 'I'm sorry, Niall.'

My instinct was right. Marlon Brando, with his poorly, gunky eyes. *Dead*. The roads are a danger here to the stray dogs, but when your eyesight is compromised, when you're almost blind like Marlon Brando was, it seemed inevitable this would happen.

What was incredibly unfair though, was that this had been a heartless hit and run. A car had knocked down the poor creature and killed him outright. Yet the cowardly driver hadn't the human decency to stop and check, or even move his body to the side of the road.

I told Rod to get home, thanked him for coming to tell me personally, but that I could deal with Marlon's body myself. He was so special to me. I needed to be there to say my goodbyes.

I drove straight to the place Rod had said I would find him; it was only 500 metres from where I was, and I had been planning to feed him next stop. I felt a horrible lurch in my stomach. No more times would he run up to me, no more times would I see him wolfing down his home-cooked meals, no more times would he nudge his wise snout into me, prompting me to clean his eyes.

His noble, beautiful body, mainly intact, was lying still in the middle of the road. Still warm to the touch, clearly he had only been gone for ten to fifteen minutes.

There was blood coming out of his mouth, but it seemed to have been instantaneous death from the car. I was grateful he wouldn't have had a slow and agonising departure. He looked so handsome and peaceful. Like he was dozing in the sun after a particularly decent feed. Poor old boy.

Could they really not have had the decency to move him? Treat him with some dignity?

But what I've learned since I've been here is that there is little point in being angry. I just have to fix whatever the dog problem is in front of me at that moment, be it upsetting, or super expensive, or time consuming. That's just how it is.

Feeling a little shaky, I lifted Marlon Brando's lithe body off the main road and onto the grass verge. Bubba, his pack leader, watched me the whole time, hanging his head low. The younger dogs were all playing in the background, oblivious, but Bubba knew exactly what was going on. He knew the score.

You might not believe me, but dogs are 100 per cent capable of mourning the loss of loved ones, just as we are. I've seen it before several times. Dogs can spend up to three weeks grieving, soulful creatures that they are. Bubba wisely knew Marlon Brando wasn't returning now.

I went and fetched a spade, and began the task of digging a hole in the ground to bury Marlon Brando. Unless you're a professional grave digger, you've likely never had to do this before. And the thing that always surprises me – though I've now buried many dogs – is just how much effort it takes. Creating a hole in the earth deep enough to bury a good-sized dog, especially in hot countries where it's crucial for hygiene, is not an easy task.

But I dug away until I had a hole deep enough. Then I wrapped him up in some old sheets, and then a plastic layer so other animals wouldn't be able to smell him and dig him back up.

Once I'd got him lovingly prepared as best as I could, I laid Marlon Brando, the Dogfather, down to rest for the very last time. I had picked a quiet spot far away from the road, and underneath the coconut palms where he spent his life being a nice and gentle boy who got on with everybody. I put him close to where his pack dwelled – Bubba, Daisy, Wigglebut, Super Max and Bouncy – so he would be in the company of good friends.

I foraged for some pebbles to make him a little gravestone of sorts, and I came back the next morning with some flowers and a little bone toy I'd had at home to make him a little memorial.

It stung me that someone had knocked him over and left him with so little dignity. A fine, noble and magnificent dog like Marlon Brando deserved a more fitting end to his life.

But I tried to focus on the positives. He really had a good life. Getting to the grand age of 12 as a street dog is no mean feat. He'd lived on this paradise island with his friends. He'd enjoyed mainly excellent health all his life. He'd got his food delivered – I was so happy to know that he'd not just got the kibble, but he was there when I introduced the fresh meals too. He had got to enjoy those home-cooked dinners with gusto towards the end of his life, satisfyingly licking up each and every tasty last morsel.

It was such a joy to see him happy like that.

I'd shown him my loyalty by cleaning his eyes without fail. And I hoped I was now showing him my love and respect with a proper send-off.

The outpouring of emotion and love once I shared with my followers the news of his death was totally unexpected. I didn't of course share the more graphic photos I'd taken, but I wanted people to know he had passed as everyone loved that dog, even on the other side of the world.

Somebody in Brisbane, Australia surprised me by sending me a picture they had painted of him, just using an Instagram photo. She really captured his spirit and made me shed a tear.

People left kind comments that touched my soul. Others donated cash in his name, which meant I could neuter and offer medicines to other dogs, in his memory.

I got the sweetest letters from children saying they wanted to donate their pocket money towards helping dogs, and people saying they would skip a Starbucks at the weekend and donate a fiver instead. Honestly, I could be in floods of tears all day thinking about the kindness of strangers through this whole mission.

I also used some money to feed 600 dogs around the island a nutritious celebration funeral meal so they had full bellies, just like Marlon Brando had when he passed.

Here was a street dog so special that many people were moved to tears, even though they'd never met him. Incredible.

That reaction meant so, so much to me. That here was a voiceless, homeless little street dog, who had never hurt a fly in his life and was happy just to be alive, grateful for his lot in life, and now he was being truly cherished and adored in his death. It made me realise kindness will always win at the end of the day.

I try not to get angry about the hit and run. How careless humans can be. But I found myself darkly wondering about the person responsible for killing Marlon Brando. Would that person receive the kind of love shown to this glorious dog, when it's their own time to pass? I suspected whoever it was might not have their life celebrated in quite such a way.

I still go and visit his grave, as I do Tyson's. I talk about the good stuff and the bad stuff that's going on with me, and I always remember to tell him how lucky I was to have had him in my life.

SEVENTEEN

IT'S NOT EVERY DAY YOU MEET A GOLDEN RETRIEVER IN THAILAND

A setback like losing Marlon Brando in the way we did can really make me feel low. For better or worse, there will always be another special dog in need.

I'd been looking after Giuseppe since the very start. He was a dog very much in the autumn of his life who had hung around the street vendors in the small village where I live. He was never short of a piece of chicken or some treats, but although he was a sort of communal dog, nobody was worried about his declining health. His mobility had started to go, with his back legs getting worse with old age. He was managing to drag himself around, but his distance of travel decreased to a point where he could only manage five to ten metres at best.

I spent weeks thinking about the best solution as his health deteriorated right in front of my eyes. It was breaking my heart, but I was all too aware of the care and attention a dog at that stage of his life would need. I was happy to provide it, but at the same time – with hundreds of other dogs that still needed my help – I wondered if it was a good use of my time. Shouldn't I be focusing on sterilising dogs?

In the end I pulled in one day on my bike, and the heavens just opened on me and Giuseppe. He was no longer able to drag himself in to get shelter, so as we stood there in the torrential storm I just said to him, 'I guess that's it, Giuseppe. You're coming with me.'

Vet checks and several different opinions confirmed the worst. He had fused vertebrae and wouldn't recover. It was now all about quality of life for him. We tried everything, including medicine, taking him for swims, acupuncture and gently massaging his old, sore legs. While his legs only improved fractionally, his spirits lifted immediately when I brought him to the sanctuary. We would bring him fresh food and he slept on the comfiest bed, with lots of pillows and blankets. It was like his retirement home, and he used to sit and bark at all the young dogs bounding around him. The twinkle in his eyes returned and he stayed with us for three months.

It was a lot of work cleaning up after Giuseppe and many of us put our backs out lifting him around. I'd sometimes worry if we'd done the right thing. It was only when I saw him in the last few weeks of his life that I knew we had.

Two examples spring to mind …

The first was a trolley my friend Rod made for him. It was like one of the big flatbed trolleys you get in IKEA. We lined it with soft blankets and installed a solar-powered fan, and he even had his own music in there. We used to wheel him around for walks and sit him near the humans to enjoy the food. I swear I could see him smiling in that set-up, peering down at the younger dogs and saying, 'Look at me. I was a street dog once, and now I'm the king.'

The second example was when Giuseppe passed. We all knew the time was right, so we gathered for some cake and drinks to have a little chat about his life. He was hand fed sausages and treats until his belly couldn't handle any more. He just thought he was attending the best party of his life, sitting up on his cart. If he hadn't been so busy getting belly rubs and more treats, he'd have seen a few eyes getting moist.

As he slowly passed without a care in the world, Giuseppe had one of my friends holding each of his paws, and another scratching his belly. This street dog had never known it so good. I looked into his eyes the very second he was drifting off, and I whispered that he was loved by so many people and that we'd make something special for him. That something special was Giuseppe's remembrance garden, where he's buried. We planted fresh grass, fragrant trees and flowers, and it's a place where we can say hello to him every day as we care for the other dogs.

Giuseppe had a good life on the streets. He made it to be an older distinguished gentleman, and at the end he just needed a little help to maintain his dignity and go to the other side with some grace.

There's one lovely story I just can't leave out. I first met Tina in February 2023. She arrived – like most street dogs – in a sorry state. So far, so normal. But Tina looked a little different from most Thai street dogs. She was a golden retriever.

Shackled to a short chain, there was something about this dog that reminded me so much of myself when I was in the ICU. Her body, and more importantly, her soul, were broken by relentless mistreatment over many years. She was in an absolute mess – literally covered in her own mess, poor thing, you can imagine how she smelled and felt – and generally looked horrific.

She was dozing, perhaps wondering, like I once had, whether it wouldn't be the worst thing if she simply didn't wake up. I gave her a little nudge awake and could see the tiniest faint sparkle in her eyes. This surprised me to be honest, given the state of her, I expected her to have given in. Yet she lifted her head, just like I remember doing with the nurses when I was in hospital, trying to give them a sign that actually, despite all appearances, I did want to be saved. I was in a bad way, but needed something to keep me going. I wasn't all out just yet. Tina was the same.

Even shackled and covered in her own faeces, her will to live immediately shone through. When I took her off the chain and got her into the car so we could go to the emergency vet, I knew her troubles were on the way to being over. But, exactly like my own withdrawals from alcohol and Valium, there would be a couple of weeks of serious physical pain as her body tried to re-adjust. She'd hit absolute rock bottom and had no hope for her future, but ironically, hitting that low place and being so broken was what it took to get her better. Of course, I'd inflicted my own injuries on my body and soul through years of abuse. Tina hadn't. Nothing was this dog's fault. It was awful humans who had allowed her to get in this state. It wasn't fair, and I wasn't having it.

Rescuing her wasn't easy. Let's face it, it rarely is. I'd received two messages from different travellers who had stumbled across her near a local tourist attraction. As soon as I saw the pictures that were sent to my phone I thought that she was the saddest-looking dog I had ever seen. I knew I had to get up there and save her immediately, so I went up to her with Rod and his girlfriend Jewells, by now also a good friend of mine. They have helped so many times.

What we faced was soul destroying. She was in the mountains tied on to a short chain with only a little bit of water to keep her going. This was bad enough, but her appearance was a genuine shock. I don't want to upset anyone with this comparison, but her level of malnourishment and emaciation reminded me of old films featuring prisoners of war. Her ribs poked through the skin of her chest, and you could plainly see her pelvis and hind leg bones. She was a walking skeleton.

Large areas of her body and face had lost their coat and the underlying skin had been scalded painfully raw by the beating sun. She showed signs of tick infestations and had badly infected ears. And the smell of her was truly terrible because the shortness of her chain meant she could only really sit in her own mess. How cruel is that? To leave a creature no dignity whatsoever?

It isn't an exaggeration to say she was the most miserable-looking dog I had seen in all my time working with them.

The so-called owners appeared and told me Tina was a golden retriever. I couldn't believe that what was in front of me was a member of a breed so associated with energy and beauty. Golden retrievers are rare in Thailand, and it looked from the teats on her tummy that the poor thing had had a lot of litters. Dog ownership is becoming trendy out here, and I imagine a golden retriever would fetch a lot of money, so I presume the owners had used Tina for breeding – and had now finished with her.

They gave me some sort of cover story about her being hit by a car and therefore needing to have her mobility limited to allow healing. I could tell this was rubbish and she had just been chained up and massively neglected.

There followed a pretty tense negotiation between the owners and us. They didn't want to lose face to Westerners, and I didn't want to make things too confrontational, or be deliberately antagonistic, so I said something like, 'Look, I'll take her away for you. It's going to be expensive to get her well again and you don't want to have to bear the costs.'

I think they were happy to get rid of her to be honest.

After we had got her away from that awful place tied up in the mountains, we went to the vet's. Now as a golden retriever somewhere between six and eight years old, Tina should have weighed around 27 kg. What she actually weighed was 12.5 kg, under half the weight she should be. The vet gave her a full once-over; ultrasound, X-rays, the lot. The images showed some really weird sharp stuff which nobody could diagnose a cause for. It was so strangely unique that the vet actually sent the pictures to other vets around the world for insight. Eventually they concluded that there were some old stitches inside her, and they looked strange because her anatomy had become so distorted from malnourishment that nobody had ever really seen this before.

We took her back to the sanctuary and fed her, once again feeling so grateful we have this place for this exact purpose.

But what happened next was a massive learning point for me, because basically we almost killed her with kindness. We gave her a huge meal and it was too much. There's actually a medical condition that can result if you overfeed people who haven't eaten properly for a long time. Their bodies can't cope with the food and they can actually become more sick than they were to start with.

Unfortunately, this is what we unwittingly did with Tina. We gave her poor starved body too much food and her stomach started to swell like a balloon. I hoped it would settle, but it kept going and bloated up to the point where she had to have an emergency operation in the middle of the night. A vet had to put a specially placed hole in her stomach to release all the gas. I could literally hear it coming out like the air from a balloon.

An epic fail that I won't be doing again. I'm so sorry Tina.

Even when we cut her intake down, Tina just wasn't used to having good, nutritious food, and in fact she had to have the same emergency procedure again. The bloating came under control after about two or three weeks, but it was a very worrying time. I kept thinking we might be able to build her portions up, but then she would bloat again. We were using all sorts, even human medicine for babies, to try and help her. There was talk of a trip to a specialised hospital, but luckily we avoided that and finally we started to build up the food – very slowly – and as she clearly felt better and was gaining some weight she really came alive. Her coat started to come back and her beautiful warm eyes started to sparkle.

While all that was going on, she slept right beside me. (Yes, OK, I broke the rule and did actually take her into the flat with me, because she had so closely bonded with me and needed round-the-clock care.) In fact, she slept right on top of me, draping herself on my head. She wanted to be that close! The love poured out of her immediately. She was sick, her spirit had been broken, and I don't think she had ever experienced love, whether it was from an owner or anyone. So she took the love and care I offered her and clung on to it. I imagine she was terrified it would be taken away so she wouldn't leave my sight.

Perhaps not surprisingly, she was a hit online. I think it's her face. Initially, it looked so big and sad next to her bony body and scraggy coat, but as she gained weight and life, it changed into one of those adorable faces we all associate with a golden retriever: pink panting tongue hanging out, scratchable ears lying down the sides of a face containing great big black eyes. She's now doubled her weight to 25 kg and she's loved by everybody.

To this day though, she will not go more than 50 centimetres away from me. She is like one of those videos of a duck and her chicks. If I go to the toilet she's outside the door. If I go and pick up the rubbish, she's 10 centimetres behind me. She's inseparable and she has started to grow into a beautiful golden retriever. She sits in the hammock, she's learned how to swim, she sits in front of the fan, she loves chasing her tennis balls. She is a joy to be around.

She's like the big soft golden retriever that every family would love. She's a classic dog, a big softy who loves your company.

To see the pure, unadulterated joy and happiness on her face, after being on that chain and in so much pain, has taught me something. It's taught me that you should always look forward and not look back. If you look back, her life was horrendous, brutal, lonely and sad, but now she's got everything she could ever want in life. She has forgotten the past and loves every moment of her present and she is healthy, sterilised, and has grown into a wonderful dog.

Saying all that, she's still recovering. I haven't got a plan for her forever home yet, as I don't want to saddle someone with a dog that is still sick or could end up being an expensive burden. When the time comes, I don't think finding her a new owner will be a problem. I think I have probably had about 500 offers to give her a home, everywhere from America, Europe and Australia. I suppose I wonder about her future. Her rock bottom made me think so much of mine that I guess I want her to have good things and a new start, just as I have managed.

I love Tina so dearly as a dog because she continues to get stronger, better and more full of love for others by the day. When she and I go on walks together, as she trots along beside me, she reminds me of *me*; two proud creatures who have been as low as you can go, but who have come back from the brink, and know we need to savour every single moment in the sun.

And once again, Tina has reminded me of the most important lesson of all – to live in the present.

Most people message me on WhatsApp, as they know how busy I am and that I don't have a lot of time to communicate. So when a fellow dog lover, Jules, called me, and her voice was shaking, I knew it wasn't good news. When the phone rings it rarely is.

She had been at the vet's for a routine check-up with Tina, but there had been some complications. Jules was waffling ...

'Hit me with it, Jules.'

'Tina has stage 2 or stage 3 kidney failure, she has three to six months to live.'

My heart sank. It felt as if I'd been punched in the stomach by a heavyweight boxer. 'Not Tina,' I thought. Just when she was starting to turn the corner and her new life was beginning, it was all about to be whipped away from her.

You have to be resilient with dogs, amid constant knocks, so I jumped in the shower, put on fresh clothes and thought to myself, 'Right, this is my duty now. It's smiles all around, get all the info, get a plan together and make this the greatest three to six months ever. Let's make it even longer, if possible.' The old Niall would have driven down to the shop and bought a bottle of wine and twenty cigarettes and cursed his luck, but it's not about me now. Tina needed me.

I have such a deep connection with Tina because I see so much of myself in her. Just like her, I had a chain around my neck for most of my life. Alcohol and addiction held me back and stopped me being the person I am today, in the same way that physical chain did with Tina.

We often walk through the jungle together and go about our little daily tasks as the two happiest little creatures on this planet. When you have been as low and to such dark places, and stared not only death but also a meaningless existence in the face, as we have, then the simple things are a joy.

I think I am like a comfort blanket to Tina. She is scared to let me out of her sight because she thinks things are now too good to be true. I feel the same with my own life, which is why we are so deeply connected. Tina doesn't need anything much in life. She just loves her food, her tennis balls and her human. Dogs like Tina have taught me the same about my life. Give me my flip-flops, a little sun on my back and my moped, loaded with food and medicines for dogs, and I am the happiest soul on this earth.

Tina won't be with us for long. The time that she does have I will make sure is extremely special for her. All Tina wants is the one thing she never had in her life and which she has so much to give. Love.

Tina is the classic example of a dog who lives in the moment. Yesterday doesn't matter to her. I wish as a human I also had that quality, to simply forget my past, but I also realise it has shaped me into the person I am today.

Every single morning I ask myself, 'If this was my last day on earth would I be happy with what I am doing?' When you have been in hospital dying, that question is especially pertinent. I now jump out of bed even before the alarm sounds and quickly nod in the mirror and say yes because I know I have to go and see Snoop, McMuffin, Jumbo, Tina and hundreds of other dogs in need.

If I did happen to get struck by a bus tomorrow, I would say that walking through the jungle with an old abused dog called Tina was easily the most important thing I could have been doing with my life.

I don't know how I've been lucky enough to end up in this position, looking after dogs in need and having people around the world support me and will me on. What I do know is that I am not going to waste this opportunity.

Just like Tina, I've been given a second chance in life and neither of us intends to waste a second of our time on this planet.

EPILOGUE

There's a popular turn of phrase that says life begins at 40. Meaning maturity is a good thing really. John Lennon even wrote a song with that title, but he never recorded it because the Beatles star was shot two months after reaching his milestone birthday.

For me though, I was still a complete disaster at 40. At the age when everyone else around me seemed to have the Big Things figured out – stable careers, families, financial security – I certainly didn't. Many friends my age were happily meandering down that well-trodden life path, but I was all over the place.

Frankly, I was a train wreck, having spent twenty-five years of my life dealing with depression, anxiety and addiction. I'd lost weeks at a time in bed with head fog. I'd ruined relationships, walked away from jobs, drifted across different parts of the globe. Only to find there was never any getting away from the real problem in my life – *me*.

I lost years of my life lurching from one chaotic bender to the next. I sat on my own drinking and taking drugs to numb the pain at six in the morning, ashtray brimming over from incessant chain smoking. All I would ever want was some escape from my own mind, some normality. The four hours' leave of a Valium or a Xanax. Twelve cans to just forget about life. Wine and whiskey to numb the void. Blackout drunk to pass another day. And the anxiety. Always the crippling, heart-palpitating anxiety.

Despite trying things like meetings, medicines and therapy, in the end it took me nearly killing myself through booze on New Year's Eve 2020, and spending three days in the ICU, to finally change everything. That grim episode at death's door made me realise that I wanted to live. More than that, it made me realise I wanted to live a life that actually mattered. I vowed to make however long I had in this world really count. To make a difference.

The physical and mental recovery didn't happen overnight; time and patience were required. And nor did dreaming up a grand plan. But eventually, aged 42, I got lucky and found my reason to be.

I would never have imagined that it would take a bunch of unknown street dogs in Thailand – unwanted, uncared for and unkempt – to show me how to make the most of my life. Their spirit, joy and resilience blew me away. From witnessing their brutal struggles, sheer bravery and dogged (pun intended) tenacity, I finally learned what felt like the true meaning of life.

People who follow my stories on social media see me as 'saving' these dogs, but in fact quite the opposite is true. It is them who have saved me.

Since getting sober, I discovered that it's never too late for a second (or third, fourth or fifth …) chance at life. With hard work and determination dreams can come true, and there is always reason to hope. Cling on as hard as you can to that.

As I've said, this work is an emotional business and you see the whole cycle play out again and again. While it's made me so happy to see dogs like Rodney and Tina blossom and come into their own over the last few months, my beloved dog Snoop is very clearly starting to show his age now, and his legs are slowly causing the old boy more and more aches.

Snoop, my shadow since he arrived in my life, and at times the only thing dragging me through the darkness of depression and addiction, has proved to be the one thing I feel who I can completely give my love to. (I've been a terribly bad boyfriend, but I am still good friends with all my exes, so I hope I'm not a bad person per se.) It was Snoop who taught me how to love without a fear of rejection. And to love with my whole heart.

When you suffer with your mental health, sometimes a demanding dog like my Britney (God love her) can make you feel worse. More anxious. Even though jumping up, playing, barking and crashing around the flat is of course normal dog behaviour. But when you're feeling so stressed or anxious that even someone looking at you the wrong way can send you into a tailspin, it doesn't feel great having a Britney-type character getting at you.

But Snoop never demands anything from me, he never has, he's just happy to have me there. He's now at least 12 (I can't be certain as he was a rescue dog himself, when I collected him in Dublin). His legs seem to be weakening, and while he hasn't been running around energetically Britney-style for several years now, he is always happy to plod along next to me for shorter walks. Always proud to be walking with me, whether in the streets of Dublin, Manchester or Thailand, holding his head high. Taking life in his stride.

Having been such a stable and loving presence in my life for so long, the idea of losing him is almost unthinkable. Some days are better than others for Snoop, but at the first sign of seeing his legs starting to give him trouble, I decided to make up what I like to call a 'VIP retirement suite' for Snoop. I put some rubber matting on the floor in case he needed to rest wherever he was, and I brought him blankets and some soft toys like I do for the other dogs in the sanctuary.

I know Snoop is an old boy now, and he can't be with me forever and ever. But I will make sure he's happy and comfortable and with all the food he adores, and he will know how very much he is loved and how his life, being the quiet, loyal friend he's been, has truly mattered. I will be there for him as he always has for me.

Finding genuine happiness wasn't easy. But now I know this is right for me, trying to save and improve the lives of thousands of dogs, forgetting all about money and status and possessions, and instead pouring my heart and soul into the welfare of these animals. For the rest of my life. I couldn't be more grateful for that chance.

It took me four decades to get here, so don't sweat it if you are not quite there yet with your reason for living. If I can find it, so can you. I'll be rooting for you, as will all my very special four-legged friends. Every wobbly step of the way. I hope you enjoyed reading our story and remember to always stick it out however bumpy the ride is. I promise you there's a rainbow – and a waggy tail or two – waiting at the end.

POSTSCRIPT:
WHAT NEXT?

It's impossible to know how to end this book because the work never ends. I love what I do, and am happy knowing I will dedicate the rest of my life to the bigger picture of helping more and more street dogs have better, healthier and happier lives.

Being with them has taught me so many lessons about life. The two most important ones that I've learned during my journey with them is that you don't need possessions to be happy, and you should only try to live in the moment.

I am so determined to make this mission work, I've even recently installed a couple of shipping containers on land to try and help speed up the progress. I know this might make me seem like a crazy dog man, but dividing my time between my own little apartment where I live with Snoop, Jumbo and Britney, and the sanctuary, as well as the streets where I feed the dogs, means I'm wasting precious hours in the day driving from place to place.

So I've bought these two cheap shipping containers to make sure every hour of my day is used effectively. As you have no doubt realised by now, whether drinking or dedicating myself to better things, I don't do things by halves, do I?

One container acts as a 'control centre', where I do everything dog related. Thankfully there's 4G for Zoom meetings, emailing and my social media posts, so it means I can work on bigger picture stuff, or be poring over a spreadsheet, while still having Tina, McMuffin or Snoop right next to me where I can keep a close eye on them.

I don't want to get so buried in the business side of things – which I realise is crucial for all my future plans – but spend less time with the actual dogs themselves, which is the whole point of everything. So this seemed a good plan to manage both.

The other shipping container is a place to rest my head. It's super basic, but that's my style these days. I know what's important and what's not. There's solar power, water from the well, a bathroom and toilet and a basic bed. Even on an ambitious mission like mine, without resting at all, I know I'll just get burned out and then I'd be no use to anyone. I don't want to just spend my days getting bogged down with looking after twenty sick dogs, I want to keep my mind focused on the bigger picture – how to improve the quality of living for street dogs all over the world.

I hope you will help me spread the love and keep lending your amazing support. As always, I promise to keep you posted every step of the way. And remember, wherever you are, wherever you live, look after dogs. Spend some time getting to know them, and I promise you, you will learn some important lessons in life. Just like I have.

QUESTIONS I GET ASKED A LOT

[*Note: I am sincerely hoping that by the time you pick up this book the number of dogs who are struggling will have been lowered significantly, but at the time of writing the figures are as mentioned below.*]

1. Can I adopt one of the dogs I see?

Yes. I have managed to re-home over a dozen so far. Most are in Thailand and some abroad. There is a lot of admin and paperwork involved in getting the dogs to Europe/ USA; bear in mind that it takes about four months to find a home for them here. I am setting up an adoption programme to re-home abroad, and hopefully there will be a full system in place to do this at scale. A flight for the dogs typically costs about $500 to $1,000.

2. How can I start doing something like this myself?

So many people want to help animals or make a difference but don't know where to begin. I was the exact same at the start of this journey.

You don't have to save a hundred dogs straight away. Start with one or two.

Read, follow and watch what I and other people do. I didn't know a thing about any of this less than a year ago. Everybody who does this is learning as they go along and you will too.

It doesn't have to be an all-or-nothing venture that you do in ten years' time after lots of planning and having given up your career. There is no reason why you can't do a tiny little bit tomorrow.

3. How do you afford to do this?

I'm lucky enough to have savings from when I worked in the corporate world and had my own company. Living costs in Thailand are very low and I have a very modest two-bedroom apartment and don't do much apart from the dogs. As it has grown, people have donated to help with vet trips and sterilising as that is where the costs really add up.

I'm very conscious that in the longer term, in order to save thousands of dogs I'll need to create additional revenue streams to facilitate that.

4. Can I volunteer?

Not yet. I'm not set up for it here in Thailand at the moment. I would love to have help, and I am in the process of creating a charitable foundation. When I have that ready to go, I'll have a great volunteer programme. I can point you in the direction of people who help dogs and who need volunteers.

5. Can I come out and feed the dogs with you?

At the moment it really is just me who does everything, from feeding, sterilising, vet trips, creating content and everything else. I have so few hours available in the day that I literally zip through it on my bike. As I get more set up, there will be ways to come and see the dogs with me in one central place, but at the moment my days are just too stretched.

6. How can I help now?

I don't really like shouting about donations or constantly putting up sad images as I feel there is enough of that out there already. I try to bring happiness to social media feeds, even if the stories are not always perfect, because they can hopefully show the positive in the world. There are two simple ways which are super powerful and which will directly help save dogs:

Spread the word. Just tell other dog lovers about Instagram or TikTok.

You can always donate here: https://www.happydoggo.com/

7. Have you ever been bitten or attacked?

Not badly. The trick so far has been walking away when you get a bad feeling about a situation. Of course it's bound to happen again now, after me saying I haven't so far, but I'll continue to be careful!

8. Is it hard letting dogs go?

No, not at all. In fact, for me, having dogs adopted is like winning the lottery – I couldn't be happier. My mission is to fix them and, if they are healthy, let them go. For those who come into my care as extreme cases, it can be hard to see them struggling, but ultimately I know that I'm giving them a good quality of life, where they are safe, loved and looked after.

ACKNOWLEDGEMENTS

There are so many people locally who help me on a daily basis. Rod and Jewells, who are always there on rescues. Valeria, Sybille and Jules, who help patch the dogs up. The list is endless as every single day I need to call on somebody to offer their time for free or to drive a dog somewhere or to fix the dog issue of the day with me. These are the unsung heroes who don't look for glory or money or anything in return. They all do it for the dogs.

Sean and Richard, thank you for your ongoing advice on a daily basis, and a huge thanks too to the vets, clinics and other dog foundations I work with. I couldn't do this without you.

Finally, a big thank you to Susanna Galton and the team at HarperCollins.